# PRAISE FOR *PARTNERING WITH STUL*

*"Anyone working on developing a growth mindset would benefit from this book. The strategies offered can be implemented ately. As an administrator, I can use this material to help guide teachers who need support in guiding students to own their learning. This would be a great book study or a springboard for Professional Learning Group work."*

**—Lena Marie Rockwood, Middle
School Assistant Principal**

Revere Public Schools, Revere, MA

*"The book provides a much-needed guide in developing student-focused classrooms."*

**—Marsha L. Carr, Assistant Professor
and Former Superintendent**

University of North Carolina Wilmington, Wilmington, NC

*"This book gives step-by-step suggestions on how to become a partner with students—to help them be better, and not just in your content area. Expose students to the methods in this book, and they will use them for the rest of their lives. And they will thank you for it."*

**—Nancy Foote, 8th Grade Conceptual Physics Teacher**

*"Mary Jane O'Connell and Kara Vandas have taken a courageous step in connecting the dots on several pieces of strategic research about student learning. They have provided classroom teachers with practical templates with which to apply the teacher's planning for instruction in partnering with students to build ownership for learning."*

**—Ainsley B. Rose, Professional Development
Associate, Corwin Press**

President, Thistle Educational Development Inc.,
West Kelowna, BC Canada

*"Practical, perfect for professional learning communities and independent study. An extremely rich resource for educators who genuinely want to empower students to be successful in college AND careers. The research supported strategies put forth press educators to engage in deep reflection and analysis of their personal beliefs and practices while equipping them with practical techniques to*

*engage students in rigorous, relevant ways in the classroom which translates to VISIBLE LEARNING!"*

**—Kim S. Benton, Chief Academic Officer,
Deputy State Superintendent**

Mississippi Department of Education, Jackson, MS

*"The book walks the reader through all of the steps involved in moving every classroom to a collaborative learning experience. The authors ensure that the reader (teacher or principal) sees how these concepts are scaffolded together to create a learner-centered environment . . . This is a book that gets better and better each time you read it. It drives you to take action. I look forward to making changes in my classroom using these strategies. The authors clearly have a vision of the classroom feel and the learning experiences that move students to own their own learning."*

**—JoAnn Hiatt, Mathematics Teacher**

Olathe East High School, Olathe, KS

*"The TRUST Model presented by O'Connell and Vandas captures the essence of what our most effective teachers do to ensure students are co-owners of the classroom and their learning. The authors have articulated exactly what is needed to create the engaging classroom environments we need in our schools."*

**—Karen Brofft, Superintendent**

Lewis-Palmer School District in Colorado

*"O'Connell and Vandas provide a wealth of information to educators proving that it is not only important to be student-focused and driven, but essential if students are to reach their fullest potential. In an era where we seemingly complicate things because we can, it is refreshing to see a book like this that is clearly written, driven by commonsense, evidenced by good practice, and supported with tools and clear examples to support both the teacher and learner."*

**—Russell J. Quaglia, President/Founder**

Quaglia Institute for Student Aspirations

*"O'Connell and Vandas do a masterful job of making the research on student achievement completely accessible, relatable, and immediately usable in the classroom. This book is profound in its ability to do this while putting the tools for implementation into the hands of teachers and their students."*

**—Kelley King, Principal, Education Speaker and Consultant**

San Diego Jewish Academy

*"Most of us are quick to agree that teachers shouldn't do all the work when it comes to student learning, but we're not always sure how to do that. In* Partnering With Students to Build Ownership of Learning, *O'Connell and Vandas tell us how to do that in an extremely practical and theoretical book. If you want to know how to get students to do more of the work, then you should read this book."*

**—Jim Knight, Author of**

*Instructional Coaching: A Partnership Approach to Improving Instruction*

# Partnering With Students

*Building Ownership of Learning*

*For Myer, Jack, Maddie, Kellen,*
*future grandchildren,*
*and*
*teachers everywhere who see their students as partners*

# Partnering With Students

*Building Ownership of Learning*

**Mary Jane O'Connell  |  Kara Vandas**

*Foreword by Larry Ainsworth*

**FOR INFORMATION:**

Corwin

A SAGE Company

2455 Teller Road

Thousand Oaks, California 91320

(800) 233-9936

www.corwin.com

SAGE Publications Ltd.

1 Oliver's Yard

55 City Road

London EC1Y 1SP

United Kingdom

SAGE Publications India Pvt. Ltd.

B 1/I 1 Mohan Cooperative Industrial Area

Mathura Road, New Delhi 110 044

India

SAGE Publications Asia-Pacific Pte. Ltd.

3 Church Street

#10-04 Samsung Hub

Singapore 049483

Printed in the United States of America

*A catalog record of this book is available from the Library of Congress.*

ISBN 978-1-4833-7138-2

Signing Editor:   Desirée A. Bartlett

Associate Editor:   Andrew Olson

Editorial Assistant:   Andrew Olson

Production Editor:   Amy Joy Schroller

Copy Editor:   Talia Greenberg

Typesetter:   C&M Digitals (P) Ltd.

Proofreader:   Dennis W. Webb

Indexer:   Sheila Bodell

Cover Designer:   Anupama Krishnan

Marketing Manager:   Stephanie Trkay

This book is printed on acid-free paper.

15 16 17 18 10 9 8 7 6 5 4 3 2 1

# Contents

Visit the companion website at
**www.corwin.com/partneringwithstudents**
for additional resources.

# Foreword

True North is about empowering students with the wisdom and confidence to exceed expectations throughout their school years and beyond. True North is about instilling an unwavering desire in students to own their learning, as they discover the freedom and responsibility for their choices in learning. Teachers who aim for True North understand deeply that to educate means to draw out one's potential.

These words from the Introduction to *Partnering With Students to Build Ownership of Learning* capture the essential message of co-authors Mary Jane O'Connell and Kara Vandas. Using the symbol of a compass and its four cardinal directions—north, south, east, west—their purpose is to continually point teachers in the right direction that will enable *students* to confidently take charge of their own learning journey and ultimately reach "true north." This purpose can be summed up in the statement at the center of their diagram, Teacher's Internal Compass: "I empower all students with the wisdom and confidence to exceed expectations."

But this purpose doesn't end with the teacher's commitment. It directly transfers to the statement at the center of their companion diagram, *Student's* Internal Compass: "I own my learning to achieve worthy goals." Both teacher and student must commit to and invest in this shared learning process—a dual responsibility directly reflected in this opening phrase from the book's title, "Partnering With Students."

What impresses me most about this book is its thoughtful blend of rationale, supporting research, examples, exercises, practical applications, personal and collaborative reflection, and next steps to implement the processes—all presented in a non-threatening approach. It truly points the way for educators and leaders wanting to begin shifting the focus from teacher-focused instruction to student-centered learning. These ideas are realistic and doable. To illustrate, here are a few key points from the three parts of the book that I believe are especially important to emphasize upfront.

In Part I, "Defining the Journey," Chapter 1 underscores the foundational necessity of building positive teacher-student relationships *first*. "We begin by surfacing the voices of students to understand the promise and hope offered when trusting relationships are formed and students are motivated to share the ownership and responsibility for learning." Regarding student voice, one of the most thought-provoking statements the authors make is this: "As our partners, students need a voice in all the important decisions that affect their learning and the operation and management of the classroom . . . *if students aren't active contributors of the classroom, they are relegated to passive observers.*"

Also in this chapter, the authors present their research-supported TRUST model, a framework for building collaborative and meaningful relationships with students that promote their ownership of learning. Teacher actions and learner actions appear together. One is never absent from the other. The TRUST model seeks to transform "forward thinking" into "forward doing." It is rooted in the willingness and commitment on the part of teachers *and* students to exercise a growth mindset that acknowledges mistakes as a natural part of learning. This belief system manifests in the creation of a "class credo," a flexible set of agreed-upon beliefs about learning that support collaboration, reflection, and risk-taking. Chapter 1 is so rich with ideas that I urge readers to spend as much time as needed to deeply process it.

In Part II, "Learning on the Journey," Chapter 4 opens with a powerful set of questions that educators and leaders will find worthy of in-depth discussion: *The question is not about teaching, it is about learning.* The question is: "*Did my students learn it?* Did all my efforts as a teacher result in learning for my students?" *Instead of focusing on what was taught, the focus should be on what was* learned.

The educational literature offers a superabundance of teaching strategies for effectively delivering content. Yet the authors propose the need for students to develop a "toolbox of *learning* strategies" that will enable them to know when it's appropriate to select one tool over another to advance their understanding of a particular concept or skill. Citing Jim Knight (2013), the authors point out that teaching students *how* to learn is as important as teaching students what to learn.

When students own their learning and set ambitious goals, the path may be initially unclear. However, a few roadblocks will not daunt students who have developed a resolute mindset intent on success. They will consult their toolbox of strategies or actively research alternative solutions and resources to learn and ultimately succeed. In other words, students with a personal toolbox of learning strategies know what to do when they "get stuck." They know how to seek help, detect errors, question, access resources, explore, and so on. These are skills for a lifetime of learning.

Awakening in students the belief in their own capacity to think for themselves—and teaching them the requisite skills to do so—is a primary responsibility of educators. This important chapter provides readers with practical and commonsense ways to accomplish the goal of transferring "teacher-owned" strategies to "learner-owned" strategies.

Chapter 5 showcases one of the most important components of learning—feedback. One section, elegantly titled "Nourishing Learning Through Feedback," underscores the truth that "feedback must be given appropriately and, more importantly, *received* and *acted upon* by the receiver of feedback. This applies equally to teachers and students."

The authors deconstruct the word "feedback" to reveal its layers of value in the teaching and learning process, suggesting practical ways to utilize feedback effectively in the classroom. One key distinction they make is between *immediate* and *delayed* feedback, persuasively explaining and illustrating with examples the importance of and difference between the two. They emphasize the need for feedback to include exemplars of student work or, as they are often referred to today, "worked examples" to assist students in self-assessing their own progress and determining where they need to improve. Readers of this chapter are sure to come away with a wealth of new information about the critical role that feedback, in its various types, plays in improving student ownership of learning.

In Part III, "Retracing and Extending the Journey," readers will learn in Chapter 6 how students assemble a "body of evidence" in a learning port-folio that shows to what degree they have achieved the Learning Intentions in focus. The authors present several types of reflections that students can use to assess their body of learning evidence. Pointing out the importance of reflection for teachers, the authors write: "Engaging in reflection with students regarding the effectiveness of the instructional structures and practices used throughout the unit provides meaningful evidence about what worked best, as well as potential changes for future instruction. If teachers skip this step, they are left to infer what was or was not effective based upon observations and assessment results alone."

For the students, "providing feedback to the teacher while proving learn-ing solidifies their important role in the classroom as partners in learning. In addition, it teaches them to be reflective and thoughtful learners, and ulti-mately, leads to the development of Learner Strategies. As students reflect and think about what worked and what didn't work to move learning for-ward, the learner toolbox grows."

In Chapter 7, the authors provide school leaders with suggestions for learning and planning systemic and systematic implementation. The book culminates with a very useful set of resources that includes a chapter-by-chapter book study guide; district examples of belief systems related to learning; worked examples of learning progressions aligned to Webb's Depth of Knowledge (DOK); and a glossary of terms used in the book that will help schools develop a shared language of terms associated with student-centered learning.

It has been my privilege to know and work with Mary Jane O'Connell and Kara Vandas as fellow education consultants for many years. They are true learning leaders with extensive experience in schools, genuine practitioners who understand the enormous challenges facing educators, leaders, and students today. As you are likely to conclude from your own reading of this important book, they are inspired realists who are eager to share with others what they have learned—how teachers can indeed partner with students to embark upon the challenging but exciting journey towards True North.

In conclusion, I have taken the liberty of combining two statements from different sections of their writing to sum up what I believe is their essential vision—a vision that *can* be realized through commitment, unflagging enthusiasm, and perseverance:

"The 'handoff' of learning represents the moment in the classroom when students are able to take ownership of their learning and become partners with their teacher and peers. It can only be achieved when teachers intentionally empower students" . . . "It is time to change the way we think about the role of students in the learning process. Students must move from being simply receivers of teacher knowledge to fully vested partners in constructing learning and becoming their own advocates and even teachers in the learning process."

With this book as your guide, you now have the means to turn this vision into your own reality.

*Larry Ainsworth*
Encinitas, California
November 2014

# Acknowledgments

## FROM THE AUTHORS

This book could not have been written without our shared vision and a true partnership. The clarity of our message developed over time as we discussed our work in schools, immersed ourselves in the research, and at times struggled to synthesize the information. Sharing our writing with each other for input and criticism exposed our vulnerability, but it never threatened our friendship or our dedication to the work. If anything, the feedback produced greater insight and crystalized the hope and path we offer our readers and the many students we hope to impact.

Being open to feedback is a central theme throughout the book. Feedback, whether it comes from within or from another person, is absolutely critical if improvement and learning are to occur. We are most grateful to the seven external reviewers who offered general and chapter-by-chapter feedback and helped us learn. The praise and encouragement from the reviewers and our editors lifted our spirits and affirmed the work. The critical and pointed feedback provided explicit, invaluable suggestions and surfaced honest criticisms for improvement. We embraced the feedback, analyzed it deeply, and used it to craft a final revision. We extend our heartfelt thanks to our editors and the Corwin team, and all who have supported us in this work.

We would also like to thank the many consultants, school leaders, and teachers with whom we have worked over the years who unselfishly shared ideas and materials and never hesitated to challenge our thinking. We also want to thank those who contributed valuable ideas and examples to the book, including Sarah Martin, Kaye Taavialma, Amy Cosgrove, Tara Lindburg, Andrea Knight, and Jim Baxter. They are our friends and colleagues. They inspire us. Through them, so many students have a brighter future.

Kristin Anderson must also be acknowledged. She has a knack for finding the talents hidden in people and amplifying their contributions. Over the years, she has been our friend and our champion. Her encouragement and counsel have proved invaluable.

Finally, we would like to say a special thank you to Larry Ainsworth, who wrote the Foreword to this book. He has been a thoughtful leader, colleague, and friend to both of us. We have learned so much from him and sincerely thank him for his ongoing support.

## From Mary Jane O'Connell

The core concepts for this book began long ago. I grew up knowing I would be a teacher, that I had something to offer children to make this world a better place. As a teacher, as a principal, and now as a consultant and author, I've always viewed myself first and foremost as a teacher, and I have never given up on a child. However, I have often questioned myself and wondered, "Who should be working the hardest? Who should be the most invested in the learning?" The reply was always the same: "The students." But I seemed to be working much harder and worrying more about the learning than anyone else in the room! How could I change this story?

Throughout my career, I have watched and listened carefully to ascertain how children learned. I have learned from exceptional teachers who seemingly worked their magic and made it all look so easy. I have worked with outstanding leaders at all levels and truly dedicated Boards of Education. I have read, posed questions, and searched for answers. It has been a passion of mine to unravel the teaching and learning process so students are equally if not more invested in their own learning and set high expectations for themselves. This book is a culmination of all that I have experienced, questioned, and learned up to this point in my life. The journey is not over: I will continue to learn, share, and teach because I am driven to shoot for the stars.

I must acknowledge many people. With gratitude, I want to recognize all the children I have tried to impact, including my own, who taught me much about how and why one learns. Thank you to my husband, Rick. As superintendent of one of the fastest-growing school districts in the United States, he focused on what was important for children and adults to learn and excel, and then made it happen. Because of him, I flourished as a principal, and I continue to learn from his leadership. He is my champion and partner in life. I am eternally grateful to my coauthor and partner in learning, Kara. She kept us grounded and is masterful at distilling key messages so they make sense and easily translate into actionable steps for our readers. Kara has enriched my life and my learning. Because of her, I have become wiser.

**From Kara Vandas**

Sometimes I look back and think, "I can't believe this is happening." I would never have dreamed that I would have this opportunity. I am so blessed to have been able to work on this project with Mary Jane O'Connell, and to share our vision and beliefs about student learning with the world.

I was a struggling student for much of my childhood. I experienced some teachers who masterfully moved my learning forward, and others who sent my learning into a tailspin. I wanted to be the teacher who changed the world for students who struggle, who may not feel they are the best learners. For several years, I worked to be that person in the classroom with my own students; and then I had the chance to support students by working with their teachers and leaders to make meaningful and thoughtful changes in their classrooms and schools. This book has given me the opportunity to share new ideas, established over the years through research and by learning from others, and to make good on the hope that I can be a part of making learning exciting, engaging, and even life-changing for students. It is through education that many students are able to build a life much different than they had ever imagined possible.

I want to thank Mary Jane for being an amazing partner and for asking me to work with her on this book. We have developed a true learning partnership together, and I have learned so much from her and cherish both her and this experience.

I also want to thank my husband, Mathew, and my son, Myer, for their enduring support and patience in walking through this process as my cheering squad. Without them, I would miss out on the joys of life and on the love we share.

## FROM THE PUBLISHER

Corwin gratefully acknowledges the contributions of the following reviewers:

Kim S. Benton
Chief Academic Officer
Mississippi Department of Education
Jackson, MS

Marsha L. Carr
Assistant Professor
University of North Carolina Wilmington
Wilmington, NC

Aimee Corrigan
Education Consultant
Denver, CO

Nancy Foote
8th grade conceptual physics teacher
Sossaman Middle School
Queen Creek, AZ

JoAnn Hiatt
Mathematics Teacher
Olathe East High School
Olathe, KS

Lena Marie Rockwood
Assistant Principal
Revere Public Schools
Revere, MA

Ainsley B. Rose
Professional Development Associate
Corwin Press
West Kelowna, BC

Jayne-Ann Young
Visible Learning Consultant
Cognition Education
Auckland, NZ

# About the Authors

**Mary Jane O'Connell** brings a unique practitioner's perspective to her work with educators. She has seven years of classroom teaching experience and over twenty years of experience as a building principal in year-round schools ranging in size from 450 to 980 students. Since 2007, she has served as a consultant working with teachers at all levels, building administrators, and central office staff in a variety of urban, suburban, and rural settings. Mary Jane has presented numerous seminars throughout the United States and volunteered for two weeks in Zambia to work with college professors wishing to improve their teacher-training programs. It is particularly rewarding when there is an opportunity to establish a relationship and partnership with others that leads to significant increases in student learning.

Mary Jane holds a bachelor's degree in sociology from the University of California, Northridge, and a master's degree from the University of Colorado in educational administration. She has personal experience with year-round education, opening new schools, and has implemented the principles of Continuous Quality Improvement embedded in the National Baldrige Criteria for Performance Excellence.

Sedalia, Colorado, is home for Mary Jane. In addition to being an avid reader and worldwide traveler, she enjoys winters skiing with family and friends. During the summer months Mary Jane and her husband live near Big Sky, Montana, on the Gallatin River. They are fly-fishing enthusiasts and open their home to many friends who share their passion for fishing. The O'Connells have four grown children, three grandchildren, and two Labrador retrievers who continue to keep the household buzzing with excitement.

 **Kara Vandas** is an educator at heart, with an enduring passion for learning and fostering learning in others. She began her career in education at a private school for high-need and at-risk youth. Her desire was to enable students to see and realize their true potential. Kara spent several more years in the classroom in public education as a middle and high school educator, and then transitioned to coaching and professional learning positions that allowed her to support teachers and leaders. Her current role as a consultant takes her around the country to partner with schools and school districts. Her work has taken her outside of the United States as well, to Ecuador and the U.S. Virgin Islands.

Kara holds a bachelor's degree in biology from the University of Wyoming, and a master of education in curriculum and instruction from Regis University. She has worked in K–12 education for over fifteen years, with a focus on instruction, curriculum design, using data to drive instruction, science education, learning environments, formative assessment, Instructional Coaching, Visible Learning, and more. She also volunteers as a board member at her child's local charter school, where she and her family live in Castle Rock, Colorado. She loves the outdoors and spends much of her free time with family and friends.

# Introduction: Finding True North

*A Compass for Teaching and Learning*

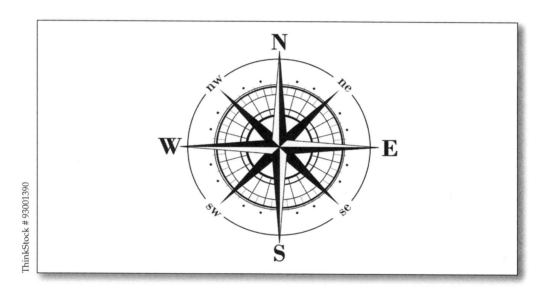

True North is the internal compass that guides you successfully through life. It represents who you are as a human being at your deepest level. It is your orienting point—your fixed point in a spinning world—that helps you stay on track as a leader. Your True North is based on what is most important to you, your most cherished values, your passions and motivations, the sources of satisfaction in your life.

—Bill George and Peter Sims, *True North: Discover Your Authentic Leadership*

As the leaders of the classroom, teachers are charged with tremendous responsibility to guide and educate students each and every year. Ask any accomplished and dedicated teacher why he or she teaches, and you will hear statements such as, "It's seeing the light bulb turn on," or "It's sharing my love of learning," or "I get to touch the lives of kids and make a difference so they can make a difference in this world!" These declarations expose the **Teacher's Internal Compass**—their passions and motivations that underpin core beliefs and values. Teaching is their calling in life.

While many teachers have found their calling in life, have they maximized their potential as *leaders of learning*, thus finding True North?

A compass is the fundamental tool to navigating any journey, and we believe there is a compass for both the teacher and the learner, enabling both to find True North. Finding True North is not simply teaching a set of knowledge and skills each year that ultimately culminates with a diploma in the twelfth grade. **True North** *is about empowering students with the wisdom and confidence to exceed expectations throughout their school years and beyond*. True North is about instilling an unwavering desire in students to own their learning, as they discover the freedom and responsibility for their choices in learning. Teachers who aim for True North understand deeply that to educate means to draw out one's potential.

Four foundational practices for teachers and learners align to the four cardinal directions on a compass. When perfectly balanced and fully integrated, these foundational practices become habits and provide an opportunity for students to be true partners in the teaching and learning process. Engaging students in this fashion has the potential to triple the rate of learning (Hattie, 2009). The journey on which you are about to travel will lead you to an in-depth understanding of what it means to find True North as a teacher and a learner. John Hattie expertly summed it up in a convincing declaration: "Visible Learning is when teachers see learning through the eyes of their students and students become their own teachers" (Hattie, 2013, p. 25).

To get a clearer picture of what this means, let's explore the four points of the compass: one compass for teaching and another for learning. When a teacher's practice is fixated on the four compass points, empowering all students with the wisdom and confidence to exceed expectations, he or she begins to see learning through the eyes of students.

The Learner's Internal Compass is fixated on owning the learning to achieve worthy goals. When a learner of any age, for any goal, can confidently answer the questions on the compass points, the learner has shifted positions and now becomes his or her own teacher. In a June 1, 2014, presentation titled "Student Voice: The Instrument of Change," Russ Quaglia captured the essence of a **learner's True North** when he said, "A student with purpose is a student with unlimited promise." Isn't this what we really mean when we strive for students to be lifelong learners?

## FINDING TRUE NORTH: THE INTERNAL COMPASSES

### Four Foundational Practices and Essential Questions

**Teacher's Internal Compass**

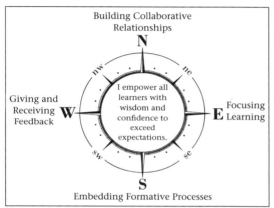

**Learner's Internal Compass**

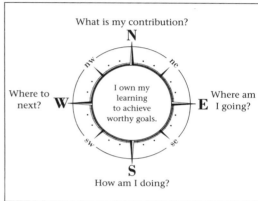

## TEACHER AS BOTH TEACHER AND LEARNER

It is critical to note that the teacher is tethered to both compasses. Teachers are the activators of learning for students and so must utilize the Teacher's Internal Compass to ensure that students are being provided with the greatest opportunity possible to realize their goals and to find their True North. However, the teacher must also be a learner; and before exploring the learning with students, he or she must be able to answer the questions linked to the Learner's Internal Compass.

## STUDENTS AS BOTH TEACHER AND LEARNER

Students too are tethered to both compasses. As they work to answer the four questions from the Learner's Internal Compass, they also provide a great deal of learning for others, both teachers and other students, and so align to the Teacher's Internal Compass. If we have done our job in partnering with students to build ownership of learning, then both compasses will be realized for teachers and learners.

## BEGINNING THE EXPEDITION

Alone we can do so little; together we can do so much.

—Helen Keller

Two highly competitive men—Frederick A. Cook and Robert E. Peary, both full of conviction and passion—were simultaneously obsessed with leading their own expeditions to find True North in 1909. Given the harsh conditions and relatively primitive navigational tools, each expedition's survival and success depended on forging trusting relationships and a collective effort of the team to achieve the goal.

As it was for the two expeditions, building trusting relationships and a united team effort is just as critical to the success of students and teachers in classrooms, schools, and school systems today. The job of providing a quality education for students is a very difficult one to accomplish alone. It is the team effort that hinges on the strength of relationships between the teacher and the students in each classroom and among the adults in the building. And yet it is what happens with one student at a time, one teacher at a time, one classroom at a time, one school at a time, and ultimately within an entire school community.

We recognize that every reader will begin this journey at a different starting point. It is our hope that you affirm many of your core beliefs and also experience some cognitive dissonance as you examine your current practices and contemplate potential changes in your classroom. Please keep in mind that building a collaborative classroom conducive to partnering with students is a process of change fraught with wonderful celebrations and insightful setbacks. It is not something that happens with the snap of your fingers. You will learn as much from your successes as from your missteps. It is all about learning, analyzing your impact on students, and adjusting your strategies that can ultimately alter your beliefs. Fortunately, when you invite the students on this journey, they will become your greatest allies, and you will learn as much or more from them as they will learn from you. They are your partners on this learning expedition.

As you engage in and interact with this book, we will expose each cardinal point of the two compasses to reveal how teachers successfully lead the expedition of learning with students as full-fledged partners. The book is organized into three interrelated sections that serve as signposts to navigate the journey: Defining the Journey, Learning on the Journey, and Retracing and Extending the Journey. Within each section, the chapters describe specific roles and responsibilities that can be shared between the teacher and the student and align to the natural teaching and learning cycle, thus providing a *road map* for partnering with students to build ownership of learning.

## CHAPTER DESCRIPTIONS

### PART I: Defining the Journey

Chapter 1: *Defining Collaborative Relationships for Learning* illuminates the beliefs and behaviors associated with positive teacher–student relationships essential to creating a culture that accelerates student learning.

Chapter 2: *Defining Essential Learnings* establishes a step-by-step process teachers can follow to find clarity in what is essential for students to know and be able to do.

Chapter 3: *Defining Criteria for Success* provides teachers with a process to translate the standards into meaningful Learning Intentions, criteria for success, and personalized learning goals.

### PART II: Learning on the Journey

Chapter 4: *Learner Strategies for Life* shines a powerful spotlight on no-cost instructional and Learner Strategies that can more than double the rate of learning.

Chapter 5: *Learning Through Effective Feedback* explores the often hidden element of reciprocal feedback in the classroom to establish the feedback structures and strategies that get results.

### PART III: Retracing and Extending the Journey

Chapter 6: *Retracing Evidence to Prove and Extend Learning* provides an eye-opening process in which students prove their learning by aligning evidence to the Learning Intentions as they build an awareness of what works for them as learners.

Chapter 7: *Retracing and Extending the Process: A Summary to Guide Teachers and Leaders* provides a critical review of the process and outlines a role for leaders by recognizing students as our greatest asset.

# Part I

## Defining the Journey

# 1

# Defining Collaborative Relationships for Learning

*How can relationships impede or catapult learning?*
*How do I establish a classroom where learning is a partnership?*

*A teacher affects eternity; he can never tell where his influence stops.*

—Henry Adams,
*The Education of Henry Adams*

In this first chapter, the Teacher's and Learner's Internal Compasses are oriented due North as we explore how building relationships with students and among students promotes collaboration and partnerships to ensure that learning thrives. We begin by surfacing the voices of students to understand the promise and hope offered when trusting relationships are formed and students are motivated to share the ownership and responsibility for learning. To create a learner-centered classroom clearly focused on learners and learning, we explore the TRUST Model, which is grounded in the best available research to date. The TRUST Model provides a framework of beliefs and actions that empowers teachers to partner with students to build ownership of learning. To begin the journey, the Teacher's Internal

Compass is focused on Building Collaborative Relationships, while the Student's Internal Compass orients to What is *my contribution?*

**Teacher's Internal Compass**

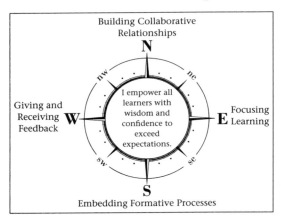

**Learner's Internal Compass**

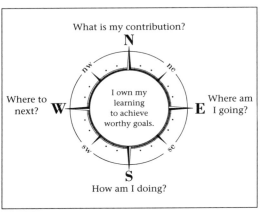

Walk into any school. Open the door to any classroom, take a seat, and spend a little time watching and listening to the students before paying much attention to what the teacher is doing. Even an untrained observer can feel the culture and climate and speculate on the health of the learning environment. Fortunately, we don't need to rely on feelings or hunches. The evidence is clear and convincing: *the nature of our relationships and our beliefs speaks volumes!*

If we *listen*, we can learn how students experience learning. If we *ask*, students might share with us their opinions and beliefs. However, should we ask, listen, and *respond with positive intent*, we might just learn more than we expected. Such is the nature of establishing collaborative relationships with students. It is a two-way street, a give and take; most important, it is an opportunity to *collaboratively* learn and grow together. To understand what we might learn from students, we begin with a sprinkling of statistics shared by Russell Quaglia at an authors' conference hosted by Corwin in May 2014:

- 54 percent of students believe teachers listen to them.
- 46 percent of students believe they have a voice in decision-making.
- 52 percent of students believe the teacher is willing to learn from students.
- 50 percent of students believe the teacher cares if they are absent.
- 56 percent of students believe the teacher cares about them as individuals.
- 53 percent of students work with adults to find solutions to school problems (Quaglia, 2014).

Quaglia shared an even less appealing glimpse into our students' world on the topic of respect. A disappointing 41 percent of students say they respect their teachers, only 32 percent of students say they respect one another, while 40 percent of students believe they are supportive of one another. These alarming statistics represent over 56,000 students in Grades 6–12. Quaglia believes asking students about their roles and aspirations and then listening purposefully can provide the venue for students to "*proactively participate* in the greater good of learning" (Quaglia & Corso, 2014, p. 1).

The Gallup Student Poll, another tool available to assess student perceptions offered to schools in the United States at no cost since 2009, is designed to spark conversations at the local school level to improve learning. This voluntary survey measures the hope, engagement, and well-being of students in Grades 5–12. The 2013 survey found 54 percent of students felt hopeful about their academic future, leaving 46 percent of students feeling "stuck" or "discouraged" about it. In terms of engagement, 55 percent of students reported feeling engaged in school, leaving 28 percent not engaged and 17 percent actively disengaged. As a measure of future success, 66 percent of students indicated they were thriving, while 32 percent were struggling and 2 percent were suffering.

Year after year, reports are issued announcing distressing statistics on the health of our schools; yet we often fail to see changes in student attitudes, beliefs, and aspirations to achieve worthy goals. Perhaps the reason stems from the mountains of survey data, which offer feedback on schooling in much too generalized a form, and not in one that can be acted upon and monitored at the local classroom or school level. Even the Gallup Student Poll results have remained stagnant over the last four years. Is there a lack of urgency or uncertainty about how to proceed? We believe teachers and school leaders are overwhelmed by mandates and solicitors, and can easily be distracted and lose direction on what is most important. We offer an approach that brings students into a partnership for learning. It is cost-free and based on the best available educational research to date. It embodies a learner-centered approach that values collaborative relationships and provides students a voice and ownership for their learning:

> This simple idea—listening to kids in meaningful partnerships with adults as a foundation for addressing youth and public policy issues—is central to learner-centered teaching, to empowering youth, and to changing many systemic inequities and failures. Meaningful change and positive growth have consistently been found to derive from supportive and caring relationships between and among youth and adults. (McCombs & Miller, 2007, p. 41)

Out of the mouths of babes comes sage advice to teachers from students in *Sent to the Principal: Students Talk About Making High Schools Better* (Cushman, 2005, p. 114). Students describe what they consider to be a fair trade to address to inequities that often occur in teacher and student relationships:

*If you* show you know and care about the material,

*then we* will believe the material can be important for us to learn.

*If you* treat us as smart and capable of challenging work,

*then we* will feel respected and rise to the challenge of demanding work.

*If you* allow us increasing independence but agree with us on clear expectations,

*then we* will learn to act responsibly on our own, though we will sometimes make mistakes in the process.

*If you* model how to act when you or we make mistakes,

*then we* will learn to take intellectual risks, and to make amends when we behave badly.

*If you* show respect for our differences and individual styles,

*then we* will let you limit some of our freedoms in the interest of the group.

*If you* keep private anything personal we tell you,

*then we* will trust you with information that could help you teach us better.

These high school students have clearly identified the heart of a learner-centered approach. Listening, empathy, warmth, respect, and high expectations are associated with the research on learner-centered practices that can significantly accelerate learning. We invite our readers to begin examining personal beliefs and practices by reviewing the descriptors used to broadly differentiate a learner-centered approach and a traditional approach in Figure 1.1. In the middle column, please place a check (√) on the continuum to indicate what you believe most typically occurs in your classroom. Consider inviting colleagues to do the same; then engage in a conversation about the specific examples that illustrate an approach that is learner-centered or one that might be considered traditional.

**Figure 1.1**   Learner-Centered Versus Traditional Teaching

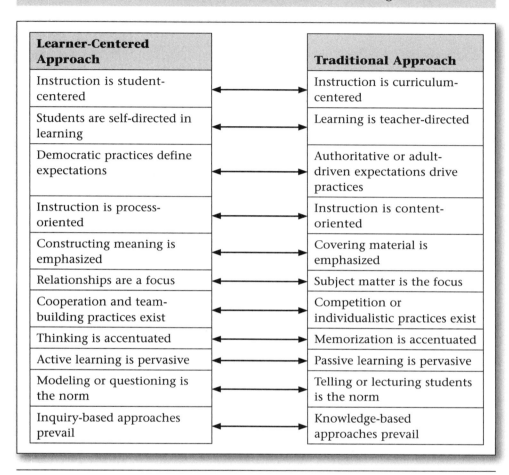

| Learner-Centered Approach | Traditional Approach |
|---|---|
| Instruction is student-centered | Instruction is curriculum-centered |
| Students are self-directed in learning | Learning is teacher-directed |
| Democratic practices define expectations | Authoritative or adult-driven expectations drive practices |
| Instruction is process-oriented | Instruction is content-oriented |
| Constructing meaning is emphasized | Covering material is emphasized |
| Relationships are a focus | Subject matter is the focus |
| Cooperation and team-building practices exist | Competition or individualistic practices exist |
| Thinking is accentuated | Memorization is accentuated |
| Active learning is pervasive | Passive learning is pervasive |
| Modeling or questioning is the norm | Telling or lecturing students is the norm |
| Inquiry-based approaches prevail | Knowledge-based approaches prevail |

*Source:* Adapted from *Learner-Centered Instruction: Building Relationships for Student Success,* by J. Cornelius-White and A. P. Harbaugh, 2010. Thousand Oaks, CA: Sage.

Before beginning any journey, it is always useful to learn about the path others have traveled to get a sense of the history and scope of the experiences that can inform a new and much-anticipated experience. Review Figure 1.2 (see p. 14) to explore some of the important thinkers and educators who propelled the learner-centered concept forward.

### Time for Application

I. The Walkabout: Taking a Deeper Look at Your Surroundings

A walkabout refers to a journey young male aborigines undertake as a rite of passage. Consider taking a walkabout in your own school as you begin your journey to learn how to partner with students. Now that your

**Figure 1.2** Learning From the Past to Bridge a New Path

Elements of learner-centered practices can be traced back to Socrates and Plato, and reemerge with educational reformers such as John Dewey, Jerome Brunner, and Joseph Schwab. Motivation to learn is activated when students are fully engaged in relevant and personally interesting processes of learning (McCombs & Miller, 2007).

In the 1950s, Carl Rogers, a humanistic psychologist, posited that a "person-centered" environment characterized by openness, empathy, acceptance, and listening was essential to human growth and development (Cornelius-White, 2007).

The American Psychological Association has reviewed the research evidence and published learner-centered guiding principles in 1997. Knowing and using the most current and reliable information on effective teaching practices to promote student motivation and achievement are part of being "learner-centered" (McCombs & Miller, 2007).

At the helm of a "learner-centered" classroom is a teacher who is relationship-driven, focuses on learning, and holds high expectations, yet also believes that errors and mistakes are expected and necessary parts of the learning process. These tenacious teachers are also viewed as being warm, caring, and empathetic. As a result, the classroom is a safe place to take risks—and, not surprisingly, learning accelerates (Marzano, 2003).

A learner-centered teacher wants to be liked by the students—not because the teacher is on an ego trip or engaged in a popularity contest, but because the wise teacher realizes that when *students like their teacher, they learn more and want to come to school*. Learner-centered classrooms can almost double the rate of learning (Cornelius-White, 2007; Hattie, 2009).

A learner-centered classroom develops a sense of community and a focus on learning among students and teachers. Learner-centered approaches create a WE classroom where both the teacher and the students are co-owners and co-learners, sharing the responsibility for what is taught and what is learned (Freiberg & Lamb, 2009).

Graham Nuthall captured how students learn and interact in the classroom by mounting cameras in classrooms and placing microphones on students and teachers. He uncovered what hides just beneath the surface and cautions us to be ever cognizant of the positive or negative contributions of students in a classroom community. "Peer interactions and social relationships are equally important and need to be carefully understood if student learning is to be explained and managed effectively" (Nuthall, 2007, p. 83).

awareness is heightened regarding a learner-centered approach and the importance of building collaborative relationships, consider actually doing what is suggested at the beginning of this chapter. Imagine you are a first-time visitor to your school and classroom. Step out of yourself and listen and look anew at the surroundings as you meander through the hallways and enter a few classrooms. What do you hear and see that suggests there is evidence of a learner-centered approach or a traditional approach, as outlined in Figure 1.1?

# THE TRUST MODEL: A ROAD MAP FOR COLLABORATIVE PARTNERSHIPS

*Although warmth describes the caring foundation of facilitative relationships, trust communicates optimistic, high expectations for students to learn and develop.*

—Jeffrey H. D. Cornelius-White and
Adam P. Harbaugh, *Learner-Centered Instruction:
Building Relationships for Student Success*

By now you may be thinking, *The discussion on theories and research is fine and dandy, but how do I do this in my classroom? I know what I want, what is important, and why it is important. I have the desire to partner with my students. I want to build stronger relationships. I want my students to believe in themselves as learners. But how? Where is the road map to guide my journey?*

In response, we have developed the TRUST Model to transform "forward thinking" into "forward doing." The model provides a framework of actionable steps and essential components supported by the research to establish students as active partners in learning.

**Figure 1.3** TRUST Model

| T | **Talent** |
|---|---|
| | Deliberate actions to discover and develop the *talent for learning* in every learner. |
| **R** | **Rapport + Responsiveness** |
| | The ability to build relationships of trust and mutual respect and to respond or react appropriately to support learners. |
| **U** | **"Us" Factor** |
| | A shared belief that everyone can learn and everyone is a vital contributor to the learning process. |
| **S** | **Structures** |
| | The methods, procedures, and practices that enable students to be partners in the learning process and to own their learning. |
| **T** | **Time** |
| | The requirement of purposeful and intentional time dedicated to building collaborative relationships and developing Learner Beliefs and actions. |

While each classroom has a different teacher and group of students, the components are fundamentally the same and critical to success. In a primary or elementary classroom, the practices and procedures surrounding the TRUST Model may appear very different from those of a secondary classroom, and rightfully so. The Model provides a framework for teachers to establish students as partners in learning, rather than a list of fun or engaging activities that might work for some and not for others. Teachers are encouraged to develop authentic interactions with students in the areas highlighted within the TRUST Model.

Although the TRUST Model in Figure 1.3 is presented sequentially to aid the readers' understanding of the acronym, the model can be entered at any point and at any time during the year.

## Talent

The *T* in the TRUST Model stands for **Talent**, and refers to deliberate actions to discover and develop the *talent for learning* in every learner. The talent for learning is encased in a set of beliefs about being smart or not so smart, capable or inept, persistent or easily dissuaded, supportive or critical of other learners, and so on. Every learner, including teachers, operates on a set of beliefs that may be obviously transparent or deeply submerged and hidden from view. These beliefs influence how a student or a teacher approaches learning and interacts with others. In the TRUST Model, teachers and students engage in deep, purposeful conversations about what it means and "looks like" to be a good learner and a supportive classmate who contributes to the learning of others. The emphasis is on surfacing beliefs and translating them into actions or **theories of practice** that can be learned through deliberate focus and practice. For many students and even adults, there is the belief that one is either born smart and learning is easy, or that one is an unlucky soul who is doomed to struggle. These theories of practice, positive or negative, envelope our bone-deep beliefs about how one develops as a learner. It is our responsibility to disrupt theories of practice that cloud students' vision to reach True North—*to own learning and achieve worthy goals.* A student's talent for learning becomes evident when he or she can confidently and expertly respond to the four cardinal points on the Learner's Internal Compass: *What is my contribution? Where am I going? How am I doing? Where to next?* We added *What is my contribution?* to complement the questions Hattie first described in *Visible Learning.* This type of talent development has been shown to double and even triple the rate of learning (Cornelius-White & Harbaugh, 2010; Hattie 2009, 2012).

Developing talent is not to be confused with acknowledging or promoting a special ability, aptitude, or flair that sets one apart from others, such as a passion for World War II airplanes, musical or physical specialties, or even an IQ in the gifted range. Although it's important to know about any specialized abilities or interests students bring to the classroom, this knowledge is more applicable to rapport-building and instructional design than to the development of talent in the TRUST Model. Talent exists within all of us, as our brains were made for learning. *Each student has a talent for learning, and it is our job as teachers to unleash it.*

Take a moment to examine a sample of potential actions a teacher and a learner might consider as a guide to developing the talent for learning in Figure 1.4. In the first column, you will need to refer to the Teacher's and Learner's Internal Compasses to indicate the cardinal direction being emphasized in the teacher and learner actions. Looking at the first two examples, you will note that a *T* indicates that the cardinal point emphasized on the Teacher's Internal Compass Is *East: Focusing Learning.* The learner's actions indicate that the Learner's Internal Compass is also pointing *East: Where am I going?* For each paired teacher action and learner action, identify the cardinal direction and corresponding practice for each paired statement. We hope that you will continue to add to the list of possible actions and share your ideas and artifacts with others embarking on this journey.

**Figure 1.4** TRUST Model: Developing Talent

**Teacher's Internal Compass**

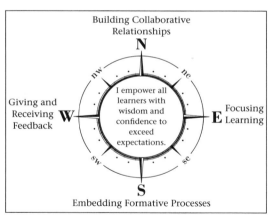

**Learner's Internal Compass**

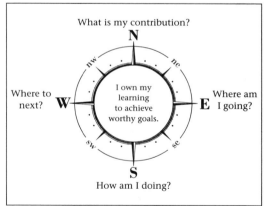

| Teacher's (T) and Learner's (L) Internal Compass Points Emphasized | Teacher Actions | Learner Actions |
|---|---|---|
| T: Focusing learning<br>L: What is my contribution? | Intentionally plan experiences that allow students to highlight and reflect on their own beliefs that develop talents for learning. | Reflect verbally and in writing their strengths as learners. |

*(Continued)*

**Figure 1.4** (Continued)

| Teacher's (T) and Learner's (L) Internal Compass Points Emphasized | Teacher Actions | Learner Actions |
|---|---|---|
| T: Giving and Receiving Feedback<br>L: How am I/are we doing? | Call attention to Learner Beliefs being expressed or developed as students engage in learning. | Provide feedback to other students and the teacher about the strengths in the classroom that exist around Learner Beliefs. |
| *Your turn . . .*<br>T:<br>L: | Post and discuss frequently the talent for learning as students progress through the Learner's Internal Compass points: *What is my contribution? Where am I going? How am I doing? Where to next?* | Identify areas for growth, based on what is valued in a partnership that focuses on learning. |
| T:<br>L: | Provide opportunities for every student to contribute to the learning of peers and others in the school. | Establish the Learner Beliefs in student-friendly terms that will be a part of the personal and Class Credo. |
| T:<br>L: | Solicit from students what is valued in a partnership that focuses on learning. | Reach consensus to adopt a Class Credo that might be periodically revised. |

### Surfacing the Talent of Learners: How Can Beliefs Affect Learning?

Just as teachers have theories of practice that guide conscious and unconscious acts, so do students. By examining how we interact with students, we can positively disrupt patterns of behavior and beliefs about learning that can have far-reaching impacts on students and teachers. A learner-centered classroom shatters preconceived limits and boundaries, and by nature, grows the minds and attitudes of all students.

The work of Carol Dweck (2007) has significantly challenged the way we think and talk about intelligence and motivation to learn. At the heart of the debate is the age-old nature versus nurture dichotomy: *Are we born with innate intelligence, or can our intellect be nurtured, developed, and changed over time? What do you believe about the nature of intelligence? How do you translate your beliefs into action in your classroom or school? Are your practices consistent with what you believe to be true?*

If we believe we are born with a certain amount of intelligence that defines or limits how much we are able to learn and achieve, then Dweck would argue that this is a **fixed mindset**. However, if we believe that intelligence is malleable and can be developed as a result of effort and hard work, then she would consider this belief a **growth mindset**. Our core beliefs about the nature of intelligence are communicated every day through our words and actions, and can have intentional or unintended consequences, depending on our level of awareness. Consider the following two statements and think about what is being subtly communicated to the student:

- *You're really smart. You were able to solve all the problems correctly.*
- *I noticed that you tried several different strategies to solve the problem and stuck with the challenge.*

The first statement is an example of a comment that can unknowingly support a fixed mindset. Although the intention is to compliment the student and reinforce his or her sense of self, statements of this nature can actually backfire. Contrary to what one might expect, by praising personal attributes such as intelligence, "You're so smart" can negatively affect a student's motivation to seek challenges. Students will simply play it safe and sometimes even resort to cheating rather than risk failing (Dweck, 2007).

The second statement illustrates a type of comment that supports a growth mindset. When praise is used to provide specific feedback on

> Teachers and leaders should send messages that intelligence is fluid, and they need to hear such messages too. They, too, need permission to learn—the freedom to stretch themselves, make mistakes, and try again. Only in growth mindset cultures, where teachers and administrators are encouraged to fulfill their potential, will they be able to help their students fulfill *their* potential in schools that are free of bias. (Dweck, 2006, p. 4)

what the student has learned and the effort he or she has expended, the student begins to believe that hard work and perseverance help grow intelligence. This type of feedback can guide students to develop a growth mindset that will lead to greater investment in learning and higher achievement; and, of course, it supports students in uncovering their own talents for learning.

In Figure 1.5, study the characteristics associated with a fixed or a growth mindset and think about yourself first as the *teacher*, then as a teacher *learning something new*. Finally, consider the following:

- To which of the following characteristics do you most align, and why?
- Is there a difference in the characteristics when you think about how you approach teaching as opposed to attending professional learning opportunities?
- Which of your students exhibit the characteristics associated with a fixed mindset or a growth mindset?

**Figure 1.5**  Characteristics of Fixed Versus Growth Mindsets

| Fixed Mindset | Growth Mindset |
|---|---|
| • Care a lot about whether others think they are smart or not smart<br>• Avoid learning challenges where they might make mistakes<br>• Feel criticism or feedback can threaten personal identity<br>• Think feeling smart, dumb, dull, or even awkward won't change even with hard work<br>• Try to hide mistakes rather than trying to correct them<br>• Believe that if they have the ability, they shouldn't need to try so hard<br>• Believe that needing to apply a lot of effort means they are not so smart<br>• Don't deal well with frustration and setbacks, sometimes giving up, cheating, or lying | • Care about and invest in learning<br>• Believe that effort is a positive thing, causing intelligence to grow<br>• Thrive on feedback and coaching to become better at a skill or learning<br>• Have an accurate perception about what they know or don't know<br>• Try hard in the face of criticism, frustration, and failure<br>• Look for new learning strategies<br>• Find that challenges spark interest and a desire to explore new opportunities<br>• Love to learn and try new things<br>• Know that practice, practice, practice makes perfect<br>• Are inspired by the success of others |

- How might you teach your students about mindsets to surface Learner Belief statements illustrative of the two mindsets?
- Several videos discussing Carol Dweck's work can be found at www.corwin.com/partneringwithstudents.

### Delving Deeper Into Learner Beliefs

Awareness of your own mindset and theories of practice regarding the nature of intelligence may have been raised a notch or two. Becoming self-aware and conscious of your beliefs and the impact of your actions on students' learning is a step in the right direction and foundational to aiming for True North for yourself and your students. These small steps can help you and your students exceed expectations with confidence and achieve truly worthy goals. It is our position that your students as partners can serve as your coaches to help you grow and learn alongside them. We know that beliefs influence how we teach and learn, and yet *changes in our practices can change our beliefs*.

In 2009, the largest body of research ever assembled in education was published under the title *Visible Learning: A Synthesis of Over 800 Meta-Analyses Relating to Achievement,* by John Hattie. Hattie and his team combed through more than twenty years of research representing over 236 million students in order to determine what has the greatest effects on student learning. He maintains that the quality of teaching and the beliefs of educators can significantly impact student learning. These beliefs or theories of practice are described as **mind frames** that

> underpin our every action and decision in a school; it is a belief that we are evaluators, change agents, adaptive learning experts, seekers of feedback about our impact, engaged in dialogue and challenge, and developers of trust with all, and that we see opportunity in error, and are keen to spread the message about the power, fun, and impact that we have on learning. (Hattie, 2012, p. 159)

The mind frames provide concrete examples of a growth mindset and a learner-centered approach. To gain greater insight and understanding of the mind frames, review Figure 1.6.

**Figure 1.6**  Teacher and Leader Mind Frame Statements

**Mind Frames**

**Teachers and Leaders**

- ✓ believe their fundamental task is to evaluate the effect of their teaching on students' learning and achievement
- ✓ accept that success and failure in student learning are about what they, as teachers or leaders, did or did not do—we are change agents!
- ✓ want to talk more about the learning than the teaching
- ✓ see assessment as feedback about their impact
- ✓ engage in dialogue, not monologue
- ✓ enjoy the challenge and never retreat to "doing their best"
- ✓ believe that it is their role to develop positive relationships in classrooms/ staffrooms
- ✓ inform all about the language of learning
- ✓ see learning as hard work

*Source:* Adapted from Cognition Education and Corwin Press, Visible Learning Foundation Seminar, Thousand Oaks, CA, 2013.

While teacher and leader mind frames or mindsets are critical to developing one's practice, the beliefs that students hold also have a dramatic effect on the outcomes of the learner, the classroom climate, teacher and student interactions, peer relationships, and more. We also know that our beliefs are the foundation of our actions, and in order to fully develop each student's talent for learning, we must begin with their beliefs about themselves as learners. We have synthesized key concepts from the research to create what we have coined as **Learner Beliefs**. Learner Beliefs are those beliefs about oneself as a learner that underpin one's actions.

In Figure 1.7 you will need to refer to the cardinal points on the Learner's Internal Compass to determine if the belief statement aligns with questions associated with North (N), East (E), South (S), or West (W). Circle the cardinal direction(s) you feel best aligns with the Learner Belief statement.

**Figure 1.7** Learner's Internal Compass Aligned with Learner Beliefs

**Learner's Internal Compass**

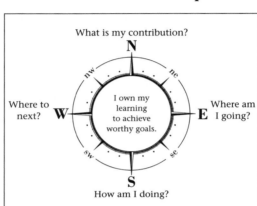

| Cardinal Direction | Learner Beliefs |
|---|---|
| N E S W | I know my learning goals and can explain how to achieve them. |
| N E S W | I seek evidence to determine if I am reaching my learning goals. |
| N E S W | I know that if I didn't learn it today, I can try a new method tomorrow. |
| N E S W | When I am in the classroom my conversations are focused on learning. |
| N E S W | I see the work and tests in my class as information to me about what I have learned and need to learn. |
| N E S W | I listen to others because I know we can learn from one another. |
| N E S W | I enjoy challenges and persist to find solutions to problems. |
| N E S W | I trust myself, my peers, and my teacher as teammates in learning. |
| N E S W | I am comfortable taking risks and know that when I make mistakes, it helps me learn. |
| N E S W | I know that learning is hard work. When I struggle through problems, I am becoming a more skillful learner. |
| N E S W | I know that I can use strategies I have learned to solve new problems or tackle new information. |

Our readers are welcome to use or adapt the Learner Beliefs. In the Appendices there are also several examples of belief statements. Appendices A, B, and C offer a set of CA²RE beliefs and practices we created for the teacher, learner, and leader. However, we believe that belief statements are more powerful when co-created with the intended audience: students, teachers, or leaders.

The following Learner Beliefs and actions were authentically established at two different schools and provide additional examples to consider. The first example, Figure 1.8, comes from Stonefields School in Auckland, New Zealand. The school has translated its learning beliefs into student-friendly actions, pictures, and words to ensure that students understand the meaning of being a "good learner." The students refer to the learner dispositions to describe their thinking and actions in the learning process. To view additional values and beliefs statements for Stonefields School, please see Appendix D.

**Figure 1.8**  Stonefields School Learner Dispositions

The second example, Figure 1.9, is from Ricardo Flores Magon Academy in Denver, Colorado. The school coined its Learner Beliefs as the characteristics that define a Magonista, or student who attends the school. The population of this school includes many Spanish-speaking students. You will notice that the characteristics of a Magonista are presented in both English and Spanish. To view the credo and additional values statements in their entirety, refer to Appendix E.

**Figure 1.9**  Ricardo Flores Magon K–8 Academy Values

**What Is a Magonista?**

**DIGNIFIED/DIGNOS**

Magonistas act with self-respect and respect others. They act with integrity and know that they will do what is right, regardless of the circumstances; they seek and speak the truth.

**UNITED/UNIDOS**

Magonistas will work together to meet their collective social, intellectual and cultural goals. They understand that they are a part of a community, and they work to educate and create a more just society.

**PROBLEM SOLVERS/SOLUCIONISTAS**

Magonistas use their logic and reasoning skills to solve all problems in a thorough and peaceful manner to create positive change.

**HUMBLE/HUMILDES**

Magonistas are willing to listen and understand that another's reasonable opinions or views deserve respect. Magonistas are generous and they always value their roots. They are confident in their abilities and in the beauty of their community, but they are never arrogant.

**DILIGENT/DILIGENTES**

Magonistas always give the maximum effort in anything they do. They never leave a task unfinished and always take ownership of an issue.

*Source:* Kaye Taavialma, Head of School, Ricardo Flores Magon Academy.

In the process of uncovering each student's talent for learning, we begin to witness how beliefs underpin actions. Therefore, by surfacing beliefs, we can begin to build accurate and growth-minded beliefs that will allow students to grow their abilities as talented learners. The following classroom applications offer some ideas about how to grow and uncover each student's talent for learning. We encourage you to take some time to consider which exercises will benefit your students, and to make plans to implement them.

### *Time for Application*

The exercises that follow provide the impetus and foundation for exploring and developing the talent for learning in the classroom. However, we encourage teachers to take these ideas and run with them.

I. Beliefs That Influence Learning

Ask students to write about their experiences as learners or what they know about themselves as learners. You might consider any of the following questions to get their ideas flowing:

- *What makes a good or competent learner?*
- *What does a learner do when confused or stuck?*
- *How can classmates/peers help our learning?*

Please feel free to share this sample with your students as a way to introduce the writing assignment, and to discuss the beliefs this author had about herself as a learner.

---

## What I Believed About Myself as a Learner

It might surprise you to learn that one of the authors of this book once believed she was a poor learner. The ideas stemmed from a negative start to school, which included starting kindergarten at a home for troubled boys. As a five-year-old girl who had not been in trouble with the law and lived happily at home with my family, this was a strange fit. Then in the first grade, I was enrolled in public school, and my teacher was in desperate need of retirement. Through many negative and frightening interactions with her, I withdrew completely, refusing to talk in class and resisting attending school at all. From these first two experiences, I believed school wasn't something I was cut out for and that I wasn't well prepared, even though I was raised in a household where learning was a priority, reading happened daily, and resources were abundant.

In the middle of my first-grade year, my parents requested a transfer to a different school to give me a fresh start. I walked into the happiest place on Earth, or so it felt. The teacher was warm and wonderful, funny and inviting, encouraging and supportive. Her name was Ms. Wardel, and I will never forget how she changed my life.

That said, even as my affinity toward school grew, my belief in myself as a learner didn't change for years. While I loved Ms. Wardel and had a series of exceptional teachers in later years, dotted with a few poor ones, my concept of how well I learned didn't change until high school and even college. I believe it is because no one ever talked about beliefs or addressed my hidden beliefs about myself; and there-fore, I spent the majority of my K–12 education convinced I was lack-ing as a learner.

From my personal experience, I can say that I wished someone had addressed my beliefs and helped me to change my thinking.

—Kara Vandas, author and educator

*What beliefs could Kara's teachers have embraced and developed in her?*

*What beliefs do you think she has now developed as a coauthor of this book?*

## II. Soliciting the Learner's Voice: Survey the Class

Consider creating your own custom student survey to learn about the beliefs and theories of practice of your students. To get started, you might modify the statements from the fixed versus growth mindset or the mind frames to create your own survey using a Likert scale that is age-appropriate. For younger students, a smiley face, neutral face, or sad face can be used to record their responses to the statements that are read aloud. Older students can use a four-point or five-point scale, ranging from strongly disagree to strongly agree, to record their responses independently. To learn more about constructing surveys and giving students a voice, refer to the Measures of Effective Teaching (MET) Project publication, *Asking Students About Teaching: Student Perception Surveys and Their Implementation* (2012), by going to: www .corwin.com/partneringwithstudents.

## III. Developing a Class Credo

The **Class Credo** is a set of agreed-upon beliefs about learning that support collaboration, reflection, risk-taking, and other important elements embedded in the Learner Beliefs. The credo can be established at any time and is a living document that should be revised as learning experiences shape beliefs over the course of the year. A Class Credo differs from developing an agreed-upon set of rules or a class contract that is voted upon and signed by all members and posted in the classroom for the year. The credo captures the evolving, agreed-upon beliefs of what it means to be part of a collaborative, learning community. It recognizes the role of every class member and the effect of his or her contributions.

Develop a Class Credo by asking students to create a list of their strengths as learners. You might ask them to make two lists in response to two questions: *What makes a good learner? What makes a good classmate who contributes to your learning?* These lists can become a launching point for a discussion to develop a Class Credo to promote learning.

How might you help the students expand and revise the credo throughout the year so that all Learner Beliefs and roles are represented?

---

Our Class Credo

Learning is job #1.
Making sure everyone learns is everyone's job.
We will make abundant mistakes.
We need each other to learn.
We all need to feel safe and respected.
We can learn from feedback from others.

IV. Metacognition: Using the Class Credo to Deepen Understanding

Once you have generated a list of learner strengths and/or Learner Beliefs with your students, begin recording examples of how each belief is demonstrated. Sometimes it is helpful to ask students to describe what the belief looks like, sounds like, or feels like in a variety of situations. Be sure to discuss negative examples and their damaging impact on a person's self-image and ability to learn (i.e., racial slurs, put-downs, ignoring someone, or disturbing others). When listening to students or observing their actions, ask them to identify the Learner Belief they are exhibiting, or one they might consider in the future. When giving feedback to students on a task, reference the Learner Beliefs to reinforce the connections to the beliefs that build a learner's talent.

*Sample Conversations*

- *As I observed and listened to the group conversation, I heard some comments that were on task and some that seemed to distract the group from achieving your goal. From our Class Credo, which Learner Beliefs can help the group stay on task and learn?*
- *After we reviewed the test, I noticed you were asking Briana questions about how she solved the problems. What did you learn about her approach? It seems to me that you were exhibiting two Learner Beliefs. Can you think of which two you exhibited? I also saw. . . . How are these beliefs building your talent for learning?*

## Rapport + Responsiveness

**Rapport** is the ability to build a relationship of trust and mutual respect. When rapport is present, students often describe their teachers as warm and caring, interested in them as a person, and someone they can count on. Rapport-building is a conscious act that is developed through shared experiences, actions, and words that communicate positive regard, unconditional acceptance, and respect. According to Cornelius-White and Harbaugh (2010), "Warmth is a way of being, something the teacher is and does, a true valuing of each student as a person." Teachers will often use humor quite effectively as a means to build relationships and rapport with students. However, this can be a very slippery slope that can sometimes prove difficult to navigate. Humor can easily be misinterpreted, or it can slip into sarcasm that might embarrass or offend others. The use of inappropriate humor or sarcasm has the potential to cripple the learning environment by causing students to withdraw to a place of safety or engage in negative behaviors that affect everyone. Ultimately, we recommend humor that encourages laughter and a sense of community, and that therefore builds rapport.

**Responsiveness** is the ability to respond or react appropriately to support the learner. A critical attribute of rapport + responsiveness is *empathy*: gaining perspective of another person's thoughts, feelings, and actions by seeing the experience through his or her eyes. It can be described as the ability to "walk in someone else's shoes" and yet remain an objective, independent observer. A responsive and empathetic teacher is able to capture not only the cognitive complexities of the task but also the emotional response of students to better inform next steps and interactions (Cornelius-White & Harbaugh, 2010). A teacher who has also established a relationship of trust and rapport will find a student is more likely to engage, accept assistance, or honestly express feelings when frustrated.

Additionally, rapport + responsiveness allows the teacher to step inside the mind of the student to determine the source of the misbehavior or learning issues to move toward a problem-solving approach. These conscious efforts build responsibility and commitment in the student to contribute to the learning of self and others. When rapport + responsiveness is modeled and reinforced, students begin to understand their role as contributing members of a healthy learning environment. Creating a safe environment to make mistakes allows students and teachers to take risks, admit errors, and work collaboratively as learning partners.

Study the teacher and learner actions you might consider as a guide to developing the rapport + responsiveness for learning in Figure 1.10 (see opposite). Using the Teacher's and Learner's Internal Compasses, indicate the cardinal point being emphasized similar to what was done in talent for learning.

### Time for Application

I. A New Twist on Student Get-Acquainted Surveys or Interviews

Most teachers are quite familiar with surveys or interviews designed to elicit information about student interests, special skills or abilities, learning preferences, and personal information. Some teachers will make home visits or call families prior to the beginning of the school year to introduce themselves and casually interview parents and students. These are all good ways to begin establishing rapport and building a relationship. Consider these variations:

- At the beginning of the year, create a social media account such as a secure webpage or Instagram. Send a postcard with your webpage information to students and begin posting information about yourself and what will be learned during the year. Continue the social media account throughout the year to invite questions and comments from students.

**Figure 1.10** TRUST Model: Rapport + Responsiveness

**Teacher's Internal Compass**

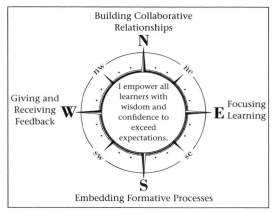

**Learner's Internal Compass**

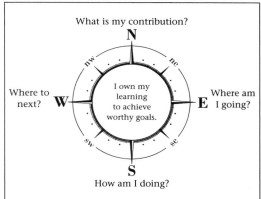

| Teacher's (T) and Learner's (L) Internal Compass Points Emphasized | Teacher Actions | Learner Actions |
|---|---|---|
| T: Building Collaborative Relationships<br>L: What is my contribution? | Develop warm, caring, and empathetic relationships | Know their classmates' strengths and preferences for learning |
| *Your turn . . .*<br>T:<br>L: | Know each student as an individual and provide opportunities for students to learn about one another | Establish and adopt the criteria for being a learner |
| T:<br>L: | Model thinking about how to demonstrate warmth, care, and empathy | Modify one's actions in consideration of a peer's needs or feelings |
| T:<br>L: | Uses rapport and empathy to diagnose learning or behavior issues | Treat others the way they want to be treated |
| T:<br>L: | Model language that promotes accepting challenges, taking risks, making errors, and persevering through the learning process | Work to develop language that supports learning as partners |

- Ask students to help construct surveys or opinion polls of any type that can be administered at any time during the year to bring their voice into the classroom.

- If your students have access to iPads, electronic tablets, computers, or even cell phones, Poll Everywhere is a great, free service that can be used to construct opinion polls, checks for understanding, and open response forums.
- Use the information you learn about your students to make personal connections throughout the year and to pair students with common interests. Consider how you can create learning experiences that capitalize on student interests.

## II. Board of Directors

To help students consider how they have developed their beliefs and what is important, ask them to think about the people who have been most influential in their lives by providing support and direction. Just as a Board of Directors is elected to help manage the life of a business, we can think of people who sit on our own Board of Directors. Ask the students to identify the people who have built rapport, modeled responsiveness, and impacted their life positively. Students can then draw a Board of Directors table and write each person's name and role (parent, sibling, teacher, clergy member, friend, etc.). Students might interview one another, share in groups, or write about these influential people and how they have impacted their lives. As students share their experiences, make connections to the Learner Beliefs and the idea of building relationships through rapport + responsiveness.

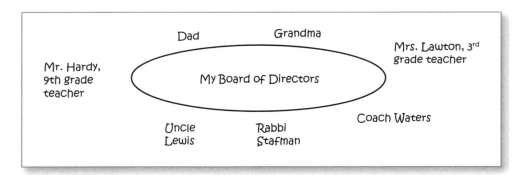

## III. Mistakes as Opportunities to Teach and Learn

- Model and share your thinking about how you handle mistakes, errors, and misconceptions as opportunities to learn. When students perform poorly on classwork or on a test, accept responsibility for not teaching the material as effectively as you might have, and share this admission with your students. Ask for their ideas on how to improve the lesson. After all, you are only human.
- Begin an "Oops!" chart or a "mistakes and misconceptions" chart: *I thought I knew . . . but I didn't. This is what I did to learn. . . .* Invite

students to share and chart their experiences along with your mistakes and insights.

IV. Use and Teach Language Strategies That Promote Learning

Figure 1.11 provides examples of specific language strategies teachers can employ that show rapport + responsiveness to students while managing them and promoting learning at the same time.

**Figure 1.11** Language Strategies to Promote Learning

| Language Strategy | Application |
|---|---|
| Acknowledge student's feelings | *It looks like you're very tired. How can I help you get this work done?* |
| Put it in writing | Write a note acknowledging improved behavior, sticking to a difficult task, or to request a different behavior. |
| Solve the problem together | *I can see you all are struggling with having your ideas heard in your group. How can we work this out?* |
| Offer a choice | *Your work can be completed in the group or independently today if you are struggling to focus. You may decide, but I need you to choose one or the other.* |

*Source:* Adapted from *How to Talk So Kids Can Learn: At Home and in School,* by A. Faber and E. Mazlish, 1995. New York: Scribner.

## "Us" Factor

Creating a classroom culture that promotes healthy social relationships is paramount to learning. As students mature and develop, their primary audience is other students, not the teacher. Teachers need to be fully aware of the peer culture: friendships, social status, music preferences, clothing choices, and so on. (Nuthall, 2007). Without a doubt, peers influence learning, motivation, and emotional responses to challenges and risk-taking. Yet teachers at all levels can create a positive classroom culture that promotes cohesion and a sense of "us." In these classrooms there is a focus on the appropriate behavior needed for all to achieve learning goals that challenge and excite students. Intentional planning along with explicit teaching and modeling can help students build the interpersonal skills needed to foster positive collaboration and social support. As our partners, students need a voice in all the important decisions that affect their learning and the operation and management of the classroom. The **"Us" Factor** promotes a shared belief that everyone can learn and everyone is a vital contributor to the learning process. Just as a coach builds a winning team, the teacher must build a team as well.

Teachers may fear giving any type of control of the classroom over to students and will shy away from allowing students to work in groups, as it can cause additional management issues. *However, if students aren't active contributors of the classroom, they are relegated to passive observers.* The question then becomes, *How do we engage students in the "Us" Factor?*

First and foremost, we must invite students to be active contributors. Next, we must work together to define their role as co-owners of the classroom. And finally, we need to put structures in place for all learners to successfully work together. In this section, we will begin by defining the actions of the learner and teacher. We have included several application ideas to engage with students and invite them to be active partners in learning. The "Us" Factor can be summed up as the team cheer, "All for one and one for all!"

Examine the teacher and student actions in Figure 1.12 (see opposite) that contribute to the development of the "Us" Factor. Identify the corresponding Teacher and Learner's Internal Compass points as you have done in the previous exercises.

### *Time for Application*

I. Community-Building Exercises

There are hundreds of books, videos, and online resources to consult for specific community-builders. Certainly, games that help students learn about one another and trust-building activities are appealing and have their place. However, our caution is to be very deliberate in selecting activities. Choose them because they build relationships to support authentic learning, and not just because they are fun. For example, a common classroom exercise is to assign students to jobs such as line leader, paper passer, and so on. Consider modifying this process to allow the class to generate jobs, roles, and responsibilities that highlight how every member contributes to the team. You might assign new roles such as advocator, wait-time monitor, questioner, or encourager.

II. Issue Bin or Parking Lot

Provide a means for students to surface issues that are affecting learning or to offer suggestions to improve the classroom environment, learning, and even your teaching. Some simple ways are to mount a piece of chart paper, provide a space on a bulletin board, or offer a comment box for students to post something on a sticky note. The teacher then screens

**Figure 1.12**  TRUST Model: "Us" Factor

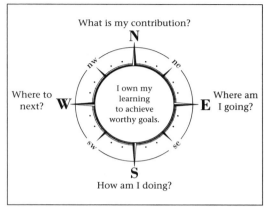

**Teacher's Internal Compass**

Building Collaborative Relationships

N

nw · · · · ne

Giving and Receiving Feedback **W** — I empower all learners with wisdom and confidence to exceed expectations. — **E** Focusing Learning

sw · · · · se

S

Embedding Formative Processes

**Learner's Internal Compass**

What is my contribution?

N

nw · · · · ne

Where to next? **W** — I own my learning to achieve worthy goals. — **E** Where am I going?

sw · · · · se

S

How am I doing?

| Teacher's and Learner's Internal Compass Points Emphasized | Teacher Actions | Learner Actions |
|---|---|---|
| T: Building Collaborative Relationships<br>L: What is my contribution? | • Involve students in generating expectations for behavior and academic expectations | • Take on role as partners in learning to support agreed-upon expectations |
| *Your turn . . .*<br>T:<br>L: | • Establish the need for a team or partner approach to learning | • Evaluate own progress toward learning goals to determine if support is needed from peers or teacher |
| T:<br>L: | • Invite students to own their own learning and take leadership roles within the classroom | • Takes leadership roles within the classroom during learning by offering assistance or support to others |
| T:<br>L: | • Activate learning while allowing students to take center-stage in each experience | • Reflect on their role as partners in learning, looking for strengths and weaknesses and setting goals in areas of need |
| T:<br>L: | • Host conversations with students to deepen student and teacher roles in partnering for learning | • Manages one's own behavior and help others manage their behavior |

the notes and decides which submissions can be discussed as a class to generate possible solutions and those that must be addressed individually.

As a teacher, it may seem a little frightening to share issues directly related to your own performance. You can certainly discuss issues with the students if they include their name with what they shared. But more important, by being vulnerable and openly sharing your students' concerns, you are modeling an important life lesson: *how to accept and act upon feedback that is less than desirable.* You are giving students a voice in their classroom and recognizing that they are important stakeholders.

Examples of student-generated issues:

| | |
|---|---|
| Ms. Finehurst,<br><br>   Do you know that you always stand on the same side of the projector and those of us on the right side have difficulty seeing? Could you please move more often?<br><br>                              Taylor | It's really hard to concentrate when some people read to themselves too loudly or other people are getting up and moving around. |

III. Plus/Delta

At the end of the class period, have a three-to-five-minute discussion with the students about the things that happened in class today that moved their learning forward (pluses) and the things that could have helped them learn more effectively (deltas: the Greek symbol that connotes changes). On chart paper, create a T-chart to record the pluses on one side and the deltas on the other. Share how you as a teacher will address any of the issues that are within your control. For example, perhaps the students indicated that they needed more examples or practice opportunities with you prior to doing independent work. The students can offer some ideas about how this might look tomorrow. Be sure to ask students to suggest what they could do tomorrow to move the deltas to pluses. On the following day, direct the students to the pluses and deltas discussed, recall the suggestions for improvement, and make a commitment. You might also ask the students to do a "quick write" describing how they will address a delta to improve the learning environment. It might be something they will do for themselves, or a way they can help peers. At the end of the period, conduct another plus/delta and you should see a significant number of the deltas move to the plus side. Be sure to call attention to the Learner Beliefs being evidenced.

See Figure 1.13 for an example of a plus/delta. The question prompts can change to solicit the information desired. For example, you might ask, "Which Learner Beliefs were evident in your groups? Which Learner

Beliefs needed to be in place in your groups?" Plus/deltas can be used daily or even once or twice a week to build and maintain the "Us" Factor.

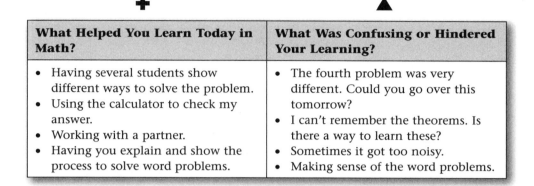

**Figure 1.13** Classroom Example of Plus/Delta Chart

| ✚ What Helped You Learn Today in Math? | ▲ What Was Confusing or Hindered Your Learning? |
|---|---|
| • Having several students show different ways to solve the problem. <br> • Using the calculator to check my answer. <br> • Working with a partner. <br> • Having you explain and show the process to solve word problems. | • The fourth problem was very different. Could you go over this tomorrow? <br> • I can't remember the theorems. Is there a way to learn these? <br> • Sometimes it got too noisy. <br> • Making sense of the word problems. |

### Structures

In the Trust Model, classroom structures are intentionally developed to support relationships and effective learning. **Structures** refer to methods, procedures, and practices that enable students to be partners in the learning process and to own their learning. Structures need to foster collaboration whether one considers the physical layout of the classroom, classroom management, or how learners work together and communicate effectively. Providing multiple opportunities for students to engage in discussion with peers develops knowledge, skills, and an opportunity to consider alternate opinions or strategies. Ultimately, working with others provides a "real-life" venue in which to learn how to resolve conflicts and disputes.

Many times the structures teachers employ involve teaching students specific expectations inherent in implementing the structure correctly. Collaborative structures that have high effect size and produce significant learning gains include cooperative learning, reciprocal teaching, problem-solving, classroom discussion, simulations, and more. These structures require the teaching and modeling of explicit expectations and procedures, just as one would teach any concept. The following instructional elements are reminiscent of "gradual release of responsibility," or steps recommended by Madeline Hunter. These general guidelines may be helpful to consider when implementing new structures:

- Explanation, elaboration, and plans to direct task performance
- Modeling from teachers including verbal modeling, questioning, and demonstration
- Reminders to use certain strategies or procedures

- Step-by-step prompts or multiprocess instructions
- Dialogue between teacher and student
- Questions from teachers
- Provision by the teacher of necessary assistance only (Hattie, 2009)

Examine the teacher and student actions in Figure 1.14 (see opposite) that contribute to the development of the structures. Identify the corresponding Teacher's and Learner's Internal Compass points as you have done in the previous exercises.

### *Time for Application*

I. Mapping Your School

Take a tour of your school and peer into several classrooms. Study their physical environment, including displays and organization, and so on. Then consider the following:

- Which rooms would you predict encourage and promote student collaboration?
- Besides the physical arrangement, are there any charts or other visuals that describe expectations or procedures for group work?
- How does your room compare?
- What do you need to do if you want to structure a classroom conducive to collaboration and partnering with students?

II. Collaborative Structures

Make a commitment to learn more about cooperative learning, reciprocal teaching, Socratic seminar, and other ways to conduct effective classroom discussions and interactions. You can find a lot of information online, including fantastic video demonstrations to get you started. Be truthful with your students and explain that you are trying something new and would like their honest feedback as you work to learn and use a new structure together. We also recommend choosing one new structure to work on at a time. As you plan units of instruction, carefully consider the types of structures that would be most useful to you and your students. Look for the right fit and take time to model, practice, and revise the structure until it works well for you and your students.

Please remember that one rarely implements a new structure or practice perfectly the first time. It takes a lot of practice, feedback, reflection, and refinement to perfect a new concept or skill.

III. Look Who's Talking

In a collaborative classroom that is learner-centered, you will typically find that the teacher does a lot less talking and the students do a

**Figure 1.14**  TRUST Model: Structures

**Teacher's Internal Compass**

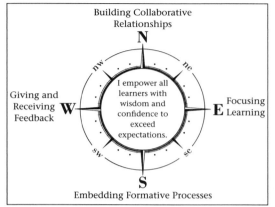

**Learner's Internal Compass**

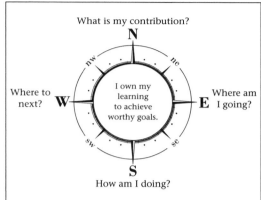

| Teacher's and Learner's Internal Compass Points Emphasized | Teacher Actions | Learner Actions |
|---|---|---|
| T: Focusing Learning<br>L: How am I doing? | • Model and teach students different ways to partner using structures for discussion, problem-solving, collaboration, reflection, etc. | • Engage in learning by practicing the structure. Provide feedback on the effect of the structure to refine implementation of the structures |
| *Your turn . . .*<br>T:<br>L: | • Establish a physical environment that facilitates learning by setting up the classroom to encourage interaction | • Provide feedback and new ideas around the physical layout of the classroom in order to best facilitate collaboration |
| T:<br>L: | • Ask for and act on feedback about refining structures to foster effective collaboration | • Persevere and try multiple ways and resources to solve problems |
| T:<br>L: | • Implement methods to talk less and listen/observe students more | • Engage in respectful, productive dialogue with others |

lot more. To get a sense of the balance between teacher and student talk, consider timing yourself to see how much you talk and how much your students talk among themselves. Track the time for at least a week. Consider asking one of your students to keep track of the time and chart it for you. If you are really serious about partnering with your students, share the information with the students and ask for their help. Once you determine the percentage of time you are talking, set a goal to reduce it and chart it for all to see. Imagine using a plus/delta to discuss the benefits of more student talk time and how the time can be used more productively for different strategies, questioning prompts, or activities. Your students will most certainly have lots of ideas. If you conduct an Internet search and enter *teacher talk,* you will be rewarded with a multitude of ideas.

### Time

The TRUST Model takes **Time**. But in the long run, it will actually produce more learning time for you and your students. The TRUST Model requires purposeful and intentional time dedicated to building collaborative relationships and developing the Learner Beliefs and actions to further learning. Time must be dedicated throughout the entire year to assess, explore, and reflect on the process of partnering with students.

As you spend time digesting the TRUST Model and how to partner with your students, know that implicit in the idea of time is the notion of practice and feedback. Practice implies lots of opportunities to make mistakes, stumble, and even fail for you and your students. But from the mistakes come rich opportunities to learn, grow, and improve: It is the idea that continuous improvement happens over time and with practice. Invite your students to share their reactions and suggestions. If you are willing to listen, admit mistakes, and try again, the students will be your guides; an idea we must embrace as teachers and learners.

Consider the teacher and student actions in Figure 1.15 (see opposite). Identify the corresponding Teacher's and Learner's Internal Compass points as you have done in the previous exercises.

#### Time for Application

I. Writing Is Thinking

Stephen King once said, "Writing is thinking through the end of the pen" (Reeves, 2006, p. 84). Take the time for you and your students to create a journal or reflection log to chronicle the journey. Provide time for students to discuss the changes in their Learner Beliefs and practices as a result of promoting greater collaboration, partnerships, and learning.

**Figure 1.15** TRUST Model: Time

**Teacher's Internal Compass**

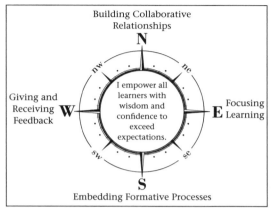

**Learner's Internal Compass**

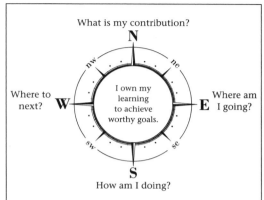

| Teacher's and Learner's Internal Compass Points Emphasized | Teacher Actions | Learner Actions |
|---|---|---|
| T: Building Collaborative Relationships<br>L: What is my contribution? | • Intentionally plan time to establish a collaborative classroom that develops Learner Beliefs within the TRUST Model | • Engage in collaboration and provide feedback on relationships, trust, and opportunities to collaborate as partners in learning |
| *Your turn . . .*<br>T:<br>L: | • Continually assess the partnership relationships within the classroom to determine next steps, solve problems, and deepen relationships and trust | • Share reflections on mindsets, Learner Beliefs, and TRUST Model |
| T:<br>L: | • Maintain a personal journal to document the journey and changes in beliefs and practices | • Create a journal to note personal experiences and Learner Beliefs |

## II. Proving Learning

In addition to collecting personal and student anecdotes, we encourage teachers and students to spend time gathering evidence of learning, finding achievement gains, and documenting effective learning strategies. (See Chapter 6: Retracing Evidence to Prove and Extend Learning.)

## SUMMING UP: DEFINING
## COLLABORATIVE RELATIONSHIPS FOR LEARNING

*Life is learning. No matter the situation, as people we are hard-wired to learn. The main question for educators and school reformers is what helps this process and what hinders it.*

—Jeffrey H. D. Cornelius-White and Adam P. Harbaugh,
*Learner-Centered Instruction: Building
Relationships for Student Success*

Maintaining a teacher-centered classroom can be exhausting work. All the energy and effort are expended to maintain control in order to manage the learning and behavior of students. As a result, it is the teacher who is working the hardest, doing all the thinking while desperately trying to deliver content, making sense of assessments, and staying up late at night planning lessons or grading papers. This is not to say that establishing collaborative relationships in a learner-centered classroom is a piece of cake. It takes thoughtful planning and time to guide students through the process to form partnerships for learning. However, once established, the classroom operates much more smoothly, as motivation, engagement, respect, and learning increase exponentially.

Throughout this chapter, we have surfaced beliefs and practices to define what constitutes a learner-centered classroom that will enable students to become our partners and own their learning. A safe and trusting, learning-centered environment is possible when teachers intentionally build positive relationships with students and among students. Our theories of practice are expressed in words and actions that reveal deep-seated beliefs. It is essential to surface and revisit them to examine our impact on students to move our own learning forward. As the lead learner in the classroom, teachers can reflect upon their beliefs and monitor their impact as they make a concerted effort to build and promote a collaborative, learner-centered classroom. With a focus on relationship-building, the teacher *as a learner* can ask of his or her students: *What is my contribution? Where am I going? How am I doing? Where to next?*

We suggest that you take time to think about potential changes in your beliefs and theories of practice as you begin to navigate the exercises in the TRUST Model. Use the reflection and planning template to make a commitment to implement one to three actions you will take and what you expect from your students as you begin to define the journey.

## Next Steps: A Template for Reflection and Planning

*How can relationships impede or catapult learning?*

*How do I establish a classroom where learning is a partnership?*

| Teacher's Internal Compass | Learner's Internal Compass |
|---|---|
| 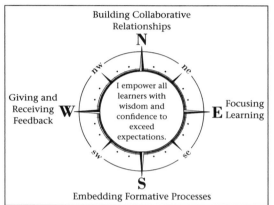 | 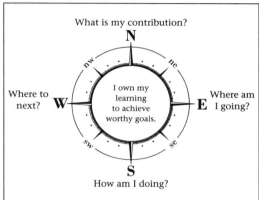 |

| Teacher's Role | Learner's Role |
|---|---|
| Defining the Journey: | Defining the Journey: |
|  |  |

For resources related to Defining Collaborative Relationships for Learning, go to www.corwin.com/partneringwithstudents.

# 2 Defining Essential Learnings

*How do I find clarity in a sea of standards?*

———————— ✒ ✒ ✒ ✒ ————————

*For students truly to be able to take responsibility for their learning, both teacher and students need to be very clear about what is being learnt, and how they should go about it.*

—Michael Absolum, *Clarity in the Classroom*

Early explorers operated under a similar question: *How do I find land on a planet full of oceans?* The plight of explorers offers educators an interesting analogy to the consuming pressure to find *clarity in a sea of standards.*

Early explorers had a definite goal in mind, just as educators do. They estimated what they would need in terms of supplies, laborers, weapons, and goods for bartering without really knowing their true needs or if they would accomplish their goal to find land, gold, or even the fountain of youth. Educators often start the school year in a similar situation, having the materials and goals but lacking direction in what to teach deeply.

While standards have become progressively clearer and more focused over the years, teachers are still faced with more than they can deeply address in a school year. Some teachers will rely on their curricular resources to guide them, and assume that if they finish the textbook, students should know what they need to know. This may or may not be the case, as some curricular resources are well aligned to the standards and others are not. Additionally, some teachers may choose to spend more time on some topics than on others, leaving gaps in what is taught and assessed from teacher to teacher (Marzano, 2003). The result is either a school year defined by a lesson a day, going an inch deep and a mile wide (Ainsworth & Viegut, 2015), or failure to finish the book—in which case standards that are addressed in the later chapters are simply not taught, let alone learned. *The bottom line is that teachers are in need of a more thoughtful approach to clearly define learning for students.* Time with students is too valuable and limited to set sail without a clear direction to define the learning journey.

It is also important to note that many experts have weighed in on the issue of finding clarity within the standards to determine priorities that will focus learning. We are faced with the same conundrum and must reach an agreement on what is most important to teach, and ultimately, for students to learn. Figure 2.1 captures some critical ideas from experts in the field of education on the need to find clarity within the standards.

Finding a clear direction and deeply understanding what students must know and be able to do sets the stage for teachers and learners to find their True North. The Teacher's Internal Compass emphasizes *Focusing Learning, Embedding Formative Processes*, and *Giving and Receiving Feedback*.

The Learner's Internal Compass highlights the path to achieving the standards. In the quest to finding True North, students must be empowered to answer: *Where am I going? How am I doing? Where to next?*

**Figure 2.1**　Rationale From the Experts

"The knowledge, skills, and big ideas learned in a class are not all equally important." (Knight, 2013, p. 32)

"Teachers need to prioritize a set of content standards so they can identify the content standards at which they will devote powerful, thoroughgoing instruction, and then need to formally and systematically assess students' mastery of only those priority content standards." (Popham, 2008, p. 36)

"Because we typically face more content than we can reasonably address, and because it is often presented as if everything were equally important for students, we are obliged to make choices and frame priorities." (Wiggins & McTighe, 2005, p. 70)

"For an educator to think it is more important to cover every standard than to focus on teaching high-leverage standards for depth of understanding is faulty reasoning. Students will not benefit from superficial coverage of standards. They will not retain what they are superficially taught, and this will necessitate the reteaching of those standards in subsequent grade levels." (Ainsworth & Viegut, 2015, p. 56)

"One of the themes of this book is how important it is for the teacher to communicate the intentions of the lessons and the notions of what success means for these intentions." (Hattie, 2009, p. 125)

**Teacher's Internal Compass**

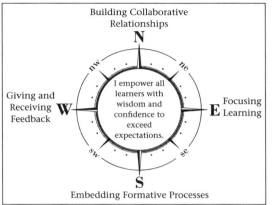

**Learner's Internal Compass**

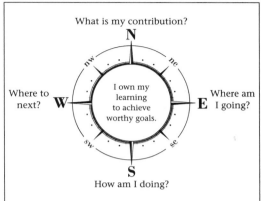

Defining essential learnings, first for teachers and then for students, is a crucial step to sharing ownership of learning with students. As previously mentioned, teacher clarity alone can double the speed of learning for students (Hattie, 2009). When students reach a similar level of clarity, the conditions are ripe for them to fully own their learning, which has the potential to triple their rate of learning. In other words, students can achieve three or more years' growth in learning in one school year. In this chapter, the emphasis will be on teacher clarity, as it must come first. In the following chapter, we will bring students into the fold as partners in learning to determine the criteria for success and to establish individual goals for learning.

## CLARIFYING THE LEARNING PROGRESSIONS WITHIN THE STANDARDS

So how do teachers find clarity in a sea of standards? To answer such a critical question, we begin with two simple steps:

Step 1: Identify the Learning Progressions Within the Standards
Step 2: Develop an Instructional Sequence

## 1: IDENTIFY THE LEARNING PROGRESSIONS WITHIN THE STANDARDS

Let's consider learning to drive a car, as most adults have endured this learning process. Even though we observed our parents and other adults drive a car and had an image of what the process entailed, most of us didn't learn to drive by setting out on a multiple-day road trip or by being handed the keys and told to "be careful." Instead, we often learned on back roads or in parking lots, and were given turn-by-turn directions from our parents or driving instructors. Our instructors thought through and planned the most introductory learning experiences we needed first. Most likely, they started with getting the seat and mirrors of the car properly adjusted and showing us how to start the car. Next, they taught us to put the car in drive, reverse, turn, shift, and other basics of handling the car. We migrated from parking lots to back roads to highways and finally to the interstate to practice and hone our skills, which provided us with a progression of learning.

The same idea applies to the standards and the **learning progressions** within them. Teachers must have a deep understanding of the standards in order to identify which standards make sense for introductory learning and which represent deep learning. One way to visualize this hierarchy or progression within the standards is to think of a scaffold used to erect a building. The scaffold has different tiers, and as one tier of a structure is completed another is added in order to allow for the next level to be constructed.

In *Visible Learning for Teachers*, John Hattie refers to this idea of scaffolding as moving from surface to deep learning (Hattie, 2012). Teachers must

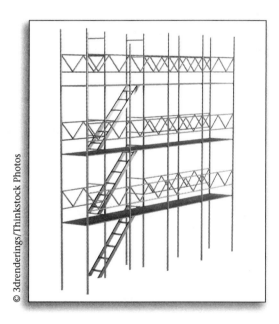

© 3drenderings/Thinkstock Photos

first be aware of what is surface learning and what is deep learning in order to understand where to begin instruction and where to take students during instruction.

Additionally, the learning progressions within standards are rarely identified within a grade level. Instead, teachers must work to determine a sequence of surface to deep learning and think through how to scaffold instruction within each unit and for the entire year. "Standards are insufficiently clear about how learning develops for teachers to be able to map formative assessment opportunities to them. This means that teachers are not able to determine where student learning lies on a continuum and to know what to do to plan next steps to keep learning moving forward. Explicit learning progressions can provide the clarity that teachers need" (Heritage, 2010, p. 39).

To apply the concept of scaffolding or surface to deep learning within the standards, we will review an example taken from the Common Core

State Standards. In the example, we will take a portion of the standards and determine the learning progression within them by using a series of questions to analyze the standards. When teachers work through the standards in this way, they can review a strand, or one logical grouping of standards at a time, and eventually work through *all* of the standards.

Within any standard—whether state, provincial, Common Core, Next Generation Science, or others—there exists a road map. The issue for educators is that the road map is not defined. Instead, standards are listed under like-topics, with little respect to hierarchy of thinking or rigor. The teacher must then determine the hierarchy, which can be accomplished by reviewing one section of the standards at a time and asking the following questions:

- *Which standard(s) in this section represents the deepest learning?*
- *Which standard(s) represents the most surface or introductory learning?*
- *If I were to order the standards, which would I teach first, and what would be the logical order?*

To best accomplish this task, it is critical for teachers to use a tool, such as a taxonomy, to determine whether a standard falls under surface or deep learning. For the purpose of our example, we will use Webb's **Depth of Knowledge**, or DOK, which was initially developed by Norman Webb to determine the level of cognitive complexity or rigor in assessment questions. DOK can also be a useful tool for teachers to examine the level of rigor in the standards as well as the cognitive demands that will be placed upon students as they engage in related tasks (see Figure 2.2).

**Figure 2.2** Webb's Depth of Knowledge (DOK)

| Level 1 | **Recall and Reproduction** |
| --- | --- |
| **Descriptor** | Recall of a fact, information, or procedure |
| **Level 2** | **Skills and Concepts** |
| **Descriptor** | Use of information, conceptual knowledge, procedures, two or more steps, etc. |
| **Level 3** | **Short-Term Strategic Thinking** |
| **Descriptor** | Requires reasoning, developing a plan or sequence of steps; has some complexity; more than one possible answer |
| **Level 4** | **Extended Thinking** |
| **Descriptor** | Requires an investigation; time to think and process multiple conditions of the problem or task |

*Source:* "Alignment, Depth of Knowledge, and Change," by N. L. Webb, November 17, 2005. Florida Educational Research Association, fiftieth annual meeting. Retrieved from http://facstaff.wcer .wisc.edu/normw/

In the sample below, DOK has been used to examine the complexity within the Common Core State Standards (CCSS) in Reading for Literature, Grade 6, into the categories of rigor from surface to deeper learning outcomes. In some cases, we divided a standard between levels, as one standard may include both surface and deep learning. By identifying the verbs in each standard and their corresponding noun or noun phrase (Ainsworth, 2010; Ainsworth & Viegut, 2015) we were able to determine the expected student behaviors and concepts within the standards and place them in the most appropriate categories of rigor.

The verbs represent a cue to the behavior expected of students to demonstrate the standard. The corresponding nouns and noun phrases provide insight as to the concepts students are learning. We must caution our readers that using charts of verbs alone can be useful but also misleading. For example, the verb *describe* can be used to signal both simple and complex concepts. Let's compare the following two standards as an example of this issue: *Describe an important event in the story* versus *Describe how two or more texts relate to one another*. The same verb is used, but when paired with the concept, a very different level of rigor is revealed. We must look closely at the behaviors and cognitive complexity regarding how students demonstrate the concept within a standard to ensure that an accurate level of rigor is assigned.

In Figure 2.3 (see opposite), you will note that the verbs have been capitalized to reveal the student behaviors expected in each standard (Ainsworth & Viegut, 2015). After reviewing the following sample, we encourage you to choose a set of standards that best fits your needs and work through the steps as explained in this chapter. In addition, a second-grade math and a high school science example are available in Appendices F and G of the book. You can also find additional resources for using Webb's Depth of Knowledge at www.corwin.com/partnering with students.

### Time for Application

I. Identify the Learning Progressions Within the Standards

1. Using a set of standards that are meaningful to you, select one section or strand of the standards.

2. In each standard, identify the verbs and the corresponding nouns and noun phrases.

3. Place each standard where it aligns best on the chart, based on the level of rigor.

(Text continues on p. 50.)

**Figure 2.3** Identifying Learning Progression Within the Standards (DOK)

←————————SURFACE TO DEEP LEARNING PROGRESSION————————→

| Standard RL.6 | Recall | Skills and Concepts | Strategic Thinking and Reasoning | Extended Thinking |
|---|---|---|---|---|
| RL.6.1 | | CITE text evidence to support analysis of what the text says explicitly. | SUPPORT inferences made from text. | |
| RL.6.2 | | DETERMINE the theme or central idea of a text. PROVIDE a summary of the text distinct from personal opinions or judgments. | DETERMINE how it is conveyed through particular details. | |
| RL.6.3 | | DESCRIBE how a particular story's or drama's plot unfolds in a series of episodes. | DESCRIBE how the characters respond or change as the plot moves toward resolution. | |
| RL.6.4 | DETERMINE the meaning of words and phrases as they are used in a text. | INCLUDE figurative and connotative meanings. | ANALYZE the impact of a specific word choice on the meaning and tone. | |
| RL.6.5 | | | ANALYZE how a particular sentence, chapter, scene, or stanza fits into the overall structure of a text and contributes to the development of the theme, setting, or plot. | |
| RL.6.6 | | | EXPLAIN how an author develops the point of view of the narrator or speaker in a text. | |

*(Continued)*

**Figure 2.3** (Continued)

| Standard RL.6 | Recall | Skills and Concepts | Strategic Thinking and Reasoning | Extended Thinking |
|---|---|---|---|---|
| RL.6.7 | | | COMPARE and CONTRAST the experience of reading a story, drama, or poem to listening to or viewing an audio, video, or live version of the text. | CONTRAST what they "see" and "hear" when reading the text to what they perceive when they listen or watch. |
| RL.6.9 | | | | COMPARE and CONTRAST texts in different forms or genres in terms of their approaches to similar themes and topics. |

4. If needed, break standards apart to best fit each portion of the standard into the most appropriate level of rigor using DOK. For example, RL.6.4 is one standard that has three parts spanning from recall to strategic reasoning.

A blank template is available at www.corwin.com/partneringwith students.

## Relationships Between Standards

Teachers can further reflect on the progressions within the standards by noticing how the standards relate to one another and how some standards represent surface learning and provide a stepping-stone or scaffold to deep learning. Learning does not always take place in a linear fashion, to be sure. However, teachers must be aware of the depth and complexity of the standards in order to thoughtfully plan for both surface and deep learning as well as the transitions between standards. "Too many innovations in education value the deep and forget it is based on the surface. One of the hardest things to accomplish in learning is the transfer of understanding. This is because deep understanding is so embedded in the knowing of much surface information" (Hattie, 2013, p. 7).

It is often the case that once a student is able to get the correct answer, we move on to the next topic, leaving the learning at the surface level. At the same time, teachers often feel pressure to increase the rigor, due to this same issue. However, without the surface learning, students often are unable to reach the most complex learning topics and ideas because they lack a solid foundation upon which to build their learning.

If we review the sample in Figure 2.3, we can see that the learning starts at the surface level, with the most introductory ideas and concepts being addressed first and then moving to the right as the standards get progressively more rigorous. As shown, the left two columns—Recall, and Skills and Concepts—represent primarily surface-level learning. As we move to Strategic Thinking and Reasoning, and then to Extended Thinking, the rigor increases to allow for connections to be made within a single text and then to include multiple texts, topics, or media.

In this group of the standards, one can identify Standards RL.6.7 and RL.6.9 as the deepest learning in the progression; therefore, students will not reach proficiency for the grade level until they have mastered Standards RL.6.7 and RL.6.9. However, we must recognize that the learning along the way is of great value and serves to support students in reaching the level of rigor required.

Looking at the standards this way can provide teachers a road map to reach the deep levels of learning within the standards by thoughtfully using the surface level as a beginning point to initiate the journey. Teachers are able to clarify the levels of proficiency students need to attain by the end of the year, while also determining which standards make sense as a starting point for learning.

### *Time for Application*

I. Solidifying Understanding of Learning Progressions

- Look over the standards you selected. Take note within the DOK chart of which standards are in the surface category and which are in the deep category. If at all possible, work with a colleague(s) to "double-check" the placement of standards to gain greater clarity on the level of rigor and learning progressions. Engaging in conversation with colleagues will clarify your interpretation of the standards and Learning Intentions for students.

- Identify which standards represent the deepest learning for the year and thus represent proficiency for the grade level.

## II. A System's Approach

Before moving on to the next step, it is recommended that teachers at the school or district level work together to determine the learning progressions within the standards. Marzano (2013) suggests that schools begin by agreeing on a *guaranteed and viable curriculum* to outline the *essential learning all students must achieve* and can be delivered within the time available. To begin the process, teachers work with their grade-level standards, moving one strand at a time in one subject area to identify and prioritize the learning progressions. Next, teachers meet across grade levels to develop the vertical alignment of the learning progressions, taking into account the balance and need for surface to deep learning. These conversations clarify the building blocks of learning that must be clearly articulated, guaranteed, and deemed doable to ensure that students meet or exceed the outcomes by Grade 12 (Ainsworth & Viegut, 2015).

# 2: DEVELOP AN INSTRUCTIONAL SEQUENCE

Once a teacher has established the progression of learning to clarify surface- and deep-learning standards, an **instructional sequence** can be drafted to plan how the standards should be assessed and taught throughout the school year. By taking the time to work through the standards in this way, teachers find great focus and clarity regarding what should be taught, which standards represent proficiency for a grade level, and how to order and pace assessment and instruction throughout the year to ensure surface to deep learning. With confidence, they can move forward to planning instruction and assessments for the school year. Without it, teachers often feel they must begin on page one in the textbook, or start with the first standard listed and teach as many as possible before the end of the year. The resulting marathon approach is neither deep nor thoughtfully planned.

Typically, teachers will find that the deep-learning standards represent between *one-third* and *one-half* of the total amount of standards for their grade level and subject (Ainsworth & Viegut, 2015). With this additional piece of knowledge, teachers can then determine a meaningful instructional sequence.

### *Time for Application*

## I. Creating an Instructional Sequence

Once you have determined the learning progressions for all of your standards for the school year, you can then begin to focus on an instructional sequence. Use the questions that follow to decipher the order of surface to deep standards you will teach throughout the school year and within units of study:

- *Does this deep-learning standard make sense to teach and assess before or after other deep-learning standards for the year?*
- *Does this deep-learning standard require multiple exposures of teaching and ongoing assessment throughout the year? If so, when?*
- *How long should I plan to teach and assess this standard and its supporting surface-level standards?*
- *How do I balance the time I have to teach with the need to deeply teach each deep-learning standard?*

Once you have answered the questions to develop an instructional sequence for your standards, you may use a chart, like the one in Figure 2.4, as a template for thinking through an instructional sequence for the year.

### *Time for Application*

II. Developing an Instructional Sequence Calendar

Take time to use the instructional sequence calendar template as a tool to work through your standards and develop a thoughtful instructional sequence for the year. Keep in mind that this process takes time and may be one that you revise several times before coming to a sequence that

**Figure 2.4** Instructional Sequence Calendar Template

| Quarter | Week 1 | Week 2 | Week 3 | Week 4 | Week 5 | Week 6 | Week 7 | Week 8 | Week 9 |
|---|---|---|---|---|---|---|---|---|---|
| 1 | Unit 1 Surface Standards Deep Standards | | | Unit 2 Surface Standards Deep Standards | | | | | |
| 2 | Unit 3 Surface Standards Deep Standards | | | | Unit 4 Surface Standards Deep Standards | | | | |
| 3 | Unit 5 Surface Standards Deep Standards | | | | Unit 6 Surface Standards Deep Standards | | | | |
| 4 | Unit 7 Surface Standards Deep Standards | | | | | Unit 8 Surface Standards Deep Standards | | | |

works well. Often, teachers will revise the instructional sequence after they have had a year to teach the sequence and gain some insight as to how it could be improved or modified.

## SUMMING UP: DEFINING ESSENTIAL LEARNINGS

Clarity around understanding the standards and what must be learned and taught begins with the teacher. Clarity requires the teacher to be fully aware of the surface and deep learning progressions inherent within a grade level. It is absolutely imperative that the teacher find clarity in the standards in order to translate clear learning expectations for students. If the teacher is unclear about what students must know and be able to do, and when proficiency is met, it is impossible for students to follow or own their learning. Determining exactly what the standards require is the first step in establishing clarity around what must be learned. Throughout the chapters, we will continue to focus on developing clarity around learning, but here we have established a clear first step. Some may ask if it is worthwhile taking the time to deeply understand the standards. The answer is a resounding *yes!* Take the time, and see the growth in students.

Use the Planning and Reflection template to identify how you will gain greater clarity on the standards you teach.

### Next Steps: A Template for Reflection and Planning

*How do I find clarity in a sea of standards?*

| Teacher's Role | Student's Role |
|---|---|
| Defining the Journey: | Defining the Journey:<br><br>*Note:* Because the teacher must gain clarity first in order to communicate learning expectations to students, the students' role comes after this initial work. |

For resources related to defining essential learnings, go to www.corwin .com/partneringwithstudents.

# 3  Defining Criteria for Success

*How can teachers translate standards into criteria for success?*
*How can students develop meaningful personalized learning goals?*
*How do we put beliefs about learning into action?*

———————— ◆ ◆ ◆ ◆ ————————

*The worst learning scenario is to be unaware of expectations or how your work will be judged and to have no guidelines about how to achieve the objective in the first place.*

—Shirley Clarke, *Active Learning Through Formative Assessment*

Have you ever heard, "Oh yes, Standard 4.3.2a; I can hardly wait!" from a student who just entered the classroom and saw the standard for the day posted on the board? We didn't think so. Yet we often expect teachers to post the standards to ensure that lessons are aligned and communicated to students. The problem is that this practice does little to focus learning, let alone motivate or engage students to want to learn. In fact, it may even demotivate them. Why? Because it is neither engaging nor clear about what is expected for learning.

In addition, this creates the typical scenario of students as passive participants and teachers as deliverers of knowledge. We want to flip that on its head. We want students to be engaged, excited, and deeply immersed in learning. That being said, we need to establish the right conditions; and to do so, we must think about how to share expectations for learning by involving students. When students begin to partner with the teacher as owners of learning, the responsibility begins to shift.

## THE HANDOFF

The **Handoff** of learning represents the moment in the classroom when students are able to take ownership of their learning and become partners with their teacher and peers. It can only be achieved when teachers intentionally empower students. You might be asking yourself, "Why is student ownership of learning so important in the classroom?" The answer lies in the research.

The typical teacher asks on average two hundred questions per day, and most of the students already know the answers to 97 percent of them. The majority of the questions tend to be at the surface level and require only short responses of three to seven words. As a stark comparison, on average students ask *one* question per day at school (Zegarac, 2013). What an incredible and troubling difference! Where is the inquiry, the wonder, the inquisitive nature of students we see when students first enter our doors as kindergartners? The brain is made for learning, for asking questions and finding answers; and yet we see many students become passive observers of learning or blatantly disengaging from learning altogether.

In 2006, Bridgeland, Dilulio, and Morison of the Bill and Melinda Gates Foundation highlighted the unheard voices of disengaged students in *The Silent Epidemic: Perspectives of High School Dropouts*. In the study, 70 percent of the respondents said they were not motivated or inspired to work hard, and 81 percent felt that if the teaching and curricula had been more relevant and engaging they would have had a stronger connection to school. At the same time, two-thirds of the respondents said they would have worked harder if the academic demands were greater, and 70 percent were confident they could have graduated. Regrettably, 74 percent reported that they would have stayed in high school if they could relive the experience.

Due to such disappointing evidence, it is time to change the way we think about the role of students in the learning process. Students must move from being simply receivers of teacher knowledge to fully vested partners in constructing learning and becoming their own advocates and even teachers in the learning process. In this chapter, we outline the critical steps to making the Handoff of learning from teacher-owned to student-owned learning (see Figure 3.1).

Mastering the Handoff of learning bears a striking similarity to learning how to run a relay race. Imagine running a relay race with three other teammates. You must run at full speed and hand off the baton to your teammate who is sprinting off before you have arrived at the point of exchange. You must slap the baton onto the outstretched hand of this moving target without dropping the baton, stumbling, or falling face first onto the track. Mastering a four-person relay takes time, lots of practice, open communication, and a fair share of stumbles before the team is in sync. You will find similar challenges in the Handoff of learning with your students. However, once students have been coached through the process and had ample opportunities to practice and refine the effort, the students and even the teacher have learned a lifelong skill.

**Figure 3.1**  Steps to the Handoff of Learning

| Teacher-Owned Steps | Learner-Owned Steps |
|---|---|
| • Uses learning progressions to determine the Learning Intentions <br> • Develops and administers the pre-assessment <br> • Provides students with specific feedback on the assessment results | • Uses the pre-assessment to determine what is known and unknown to create personalized learning goals <br> • Co-constructs Success Criteria, aligned to the Learning Intentions <br> • Includes Learner Beliefs as part of the criteria for success |

## 1. Use Learning Progressions to Determine Learning Intentions

In Chapter 2, we explored how to establish learning progressions by analyzing the standards, using Webb's Depth of Knowledge. After finalizing the progressions, teachers can select the appropriate standards for each unit of study based on the time of year, what has already been learned, and what must still be learned during the school year. While it is possible to select all the standards in the learning progression, we recommend focusing instruction on a few standards at a time so that the Learning Intentions can be clearly communicated to students, learning can progress from surface to deep, and each standard can be thoroughly assessed. Thus, we align with the direction *East: Focusing Learning* on the Teacher's Internal Compass because part of our role in partnering with students is to gain clarity on Learning Intentions that will focus learning.

In Figure 3.2, you will notice two bolded standards that specifically address plot and character development. The learning progression developed in this example identifies the selected standards as being taught *after* students are able to identify the main idea, cite text evidence to support the main idea, and write basic summaries about the main idea with supporting details. In addition, we realize that the richest units of study combine writing, speaking, listening, and other standards that connect to interdisciplinary content areas. However, for the sake of exploring the process, we have chosen to keep it simple by focusing on two literacy standards, RL.6.3 and RL.6.5. Finally, it is important to note that while we are using a reading example, learning progressions exist in every subject matter, from math to woodshop to music. We recommend that you practice the process in a way that is most meaningful to you as you study the example and then work with your own content-specific standards.

**Figure 3.2** Surface to Deep Learning Progressions

←─────────────── SURFACE TO DEEP LEARNING PROGRESSION ───────────────→

| DOK | Recall | Skills and Concepts | Strategic Thinking and Reasoning | Extended Thinking |
|---|---|---|---|---|
| RL.6.1 | | CITE text evidence to support analysis of what the text says explicitly. | SUPPORT inferences made from the text. | |
| RL.6.2 | | DETERMINE the theme or central idea of a text. PROVIDE a summary of the text distinct from personal opinions or judgments. | DETERMINE how it is conveyed through particular details. | |
| RL.6.3 | | **DESCRIBE how a particular story's or drama's plot unfolds in a series of episodes.** | **DESCRIBE how the characters respond or change as the plot moves toward resolution.** | |
| RL.6.4 | DETERMINE the meaning of words and phrases as they are used in a text; include figurative and connotative meanings. | | ANALYZE the impact of a specific word choice on the meaning and tone. | |

| DOK | Recall | Skills and Concepts | Strategic Thinking and Reasoning | Extended Thinking |
|---|---|---|---|---|
| RL.6.5 | | | **ANALYZE how a particular sentence, chapter, scene, or stanza fits into the overall structure of a text and contributes to the development of the theme, setting, or plot.** | |
| RL.6.6 | | | EXPLAIN how an author develops the point of view of the narrator or speaker in a text. | |
| RL.6.7 | | | COMPARE and CONTRAST the experience of reading a story, drama, or poem to listening to or viewing an audio, video, or live version of the text. | CONTRAST what they "see" and "hear" when reading the text to what they perceive when they listen or watch. |
| RL.6.9 | | | | COMPARE and CONTRAST texts in different forms or genres in terms of their approaches to similar themes and topics. |

Now that we have selected the standards from the learning progression, we can work to translate standards into age-appropriate, student-friendly Learning Intentions. The **Learning Intention** represents what is intended for students to learn, which is based on the standards and our inferences regarding what we believe students need to learn at this point in time.

Teachers must develop clear Learning Intentions, or expectations for learning. Figure 3.3 shows examples of Learning Intentions crafted from the standards.

**Figure 3.3** Learning Intentions and Expectations for Learning

| Standard RL.6.3 | |
|---|---|
| DESCRIBE how a particular story's or drama's plot unfolds in a series of episodes. | DESCRIBE how the characters respond or change as the plot moves toward resolution. |
| **Corresponding Student-Friendly Learning Intentions** | |
| To explain how the plot moves a story along | To describe how characters are affected by the events in the story |

| Standard RL.6.5 |
|---|
| ANALYZE how a particular sentence, chapter, scene, or stanza fits into the overall structure of a text and contributes to the development of the theme, setting, or plot. |
| **Corresponding Student-Friendly Learning Intentions** |
| To show how different parts of a story affect its meaning and the way the whole story turns out |

*"What is the intended learning?* This one question should drive all planning and assessment in schools today. Label these learning statements 'content standards,' 'benchmarks,' 'grade level indicators,' 'grade level expectations,' 'essential learnings,' 'learning outcomes,' 'lesson objectives,' 'learning intentions,' or whatever you like; they all represent *learning targets*, or *statements of intended learning*. If we don't begin with clear statements of the intended learning, we won't end with sound assessments." (Stiggins, Arter, Chappuis, & Chappuis, 2006, p. 54)

Using Learning Intentions such as the examples in Figure 3.4 (see opposite) has become more and more commonplace in classrooms today; however, it is not *that* we use them but *how* we use them that begins the Transfer of ownership of learning to students. In too many classrooms today, the Learning Intentions are simply fixtures in the classroom—*always there but rarely used to clarify or accelerate learning.* In this model, *students* use the Learning Intentions to develop personalized learning goals and co-construct Success Criteria to meet the Learning Intention—*thus reaching the Handoff, where students can become fully vested partners in the learning process.*

**Figure 3.4** Additional Examples of Learning Intentions From Literature

| Learning Goal or Intention | Text |
|---|---|
| • To learn to cut a straight line with scissors<br>• To paint in the style of Monet<br>• To know about the senses and their purpose<br>• To write a persuasive argument | *Active Learning Through Formative Assessment* (2008) by Shirley Clarke, pp. 83, 86, 88, 107 |
| • Use reading strategies together to make meaning while you are reading aloud<br>• Understand the features of desert plants and how they are adapted to their environment<br>• Understand the structure of a coordinate grid | *Formative Assessment: Making It Happen in the Classroom* (2010), by Margaret Heritage, pp. 46, 47, 49 |
| • Write a fictional narrative<br>• Given a selection of words, sort them into categories representing parts of speech | *Classroom Assessment for Student Learning: Using It Right, Doing It Well* (2006), by Rick Stiggins, Judith Arter, Jan Chappius, and Steve Chappius, p. 70 |
| • To be able to write clear instructions<br>• To know the duties and responsibilities of religious leaders<br>• To design fair tests for scientific questions | *Embedded Formative Assessment* (2011), by Dylan Wiliam, p. 61 |

*Note:* Notice that the examples from different experts in the field of education have slightly different formats but still provide students with clear learning goals or intentions.

## 2. Develop, Administer, and Provide Feedback on the Pre-assessment

We encourage our readers to rethink the pre-assessment and how you—and more important, the students—can use it. The pre-assessment provides the baseline data that will help you determine your own effectiveness as you progress through the unit; learning is growth, after all. Our growth as teachers is learning what works and doesn't work to accelerate learning in our students. In fact, one of the highest effects found in research on student learning aligns to this very idea. When teachers use assessments as feedback about their teaching, are

"But whatever you intend, in order to know if you have been effective, you must have some way of knowing what your students believed, knew, could do, or felt *before* you taught them and what your students believed, knew, could do, or felt *after* you taught them. Learning, of whatever kind, is about change, and unless you know what has changed in the minds, skills, and attitudes of your students, you cannot really know how effective you have been." (Nuthall, 2007, p. 35) willing to seek negative feedback about their own performance, and adjust instruction to meet the needs of the students, over two years' growth in learning can take place in one year (Hattie, 2009).

Another major reason to embrace the pre-assessment is so students can see their growth in learning clearly. Too often, we hear about students being unmotivated. Simply having students track their progress will build a growth mindset that opens their minds to the fact that they can learn and are learning. Motivation will boost confidence and a desire to learn more, take risks, and see their own potential. Teachers often use pre-assessment information to determine what students know and don't know to inform their instruction; this is best practice, but it is *only half of the equation*—students' understanding of where they are in reaching the Learning Intentions is the other half. It is impossible for students to take ownership if they are unaware of what they must know and be able to do within a given time frame. "Assessment is primarily concerned with providing teachers and/or students' feedback information, and needs to address three questions: What are the Learning Intentions? How am I doing? And Where to next?" (Hattie, 2003, p. 2).

## An Illustrated Example

As a school principal for many years, I had teachers who embraced the idea of students knowing how they performed on assessments, setting personal goals, and action-planning. They regularly administered the Developmental Reading Assessment (DRA) to students at least three times a year or more, depending on the growth or lack of growth in a student's reading ability. This way, students knew their reading level and the level they needed to reach by the end of the year. It wasn't kept a secret from students or parents. Each room had a rich classroom library with some books labeled using Fountas and Pinnell reading levels. Students had ample time to read independently or with peers from a wide selection of literature and informational texts. They created personal goals and action plans to monitor their reading levels and the strategies they used to advance their reading skills and comprehension. As soon as teachers in kindergarten through sixth grade began engaging in conversations with students about how to become a better reader and how to *know* one was becoming a better reader, the students became increasingly self-directed and goal-oriented. It was not uncommon for students to ask and even *beg* teachers to administer the DRA to prove their reading prowess. Before a teacher would agree to do so, the students needed to provide evidence of books they were able to read at the anticipated reading level they had set to master. *More important,* students were required to describe their strategies, how they *knew they understood* the text, and how they monitored their comprehension. We wanted to impress upon students that being able to read at a particular reading level wasn't as important as being able to use a multitude of strategies to gain meaning from reading any type of genre.

—Mary Jane O'Connell, author and educator

*Why do you think it was important to have a classroom library with only some of the books labeled by reading level?*

*What do you think teachers learned as a result of having students articulate the strategies they used to improve their reading as well as how they knew they comprehended the reading material?*

*What might you consider trying as a result of reading this example?*

To further explore the use of pre-assessment, we have included sample pre-assessment questions aligned to the Learning Intentions. You will notice in Figure 3.5 (see p. 64) that the assessment provides scaffolding, or a surface to deep progression of what students need to know and be able to do. The assessment questions begin at a level below the rigor of the standard, move to the rigor of the standard for the selected unit of study, and then go beyond to the rigor expected by the end of the school year. Using this methodology, teachers and students can see at which level of learning students are performing in order to best plan next steps and set appropriate and meaningful personalized learning goals.

Take a few moments to review the assessment in Figure 3.5, noticing how the questions align to the standards. Take note of the surface to deep construction of the assessment by referring to the learning progression chart for reading for literature, Grade 6, in Figure 3.2. We acknowledge that teachers need not select *all* of the questions provided for a pre-assessment; rather, a thoughtful sampling that best represents the learning progression is recommended. Teachers can then use the questions paired with their own text selections, based on the resources available.

After reviewing the assessment, it may be evident that some of the assessment questions overlap. That being the case, the teacher may choose to use a smaller number or revise several questions to present the question in a selected response format, which may be more efficient. It also is important to note that teachers may also select a performance assessment as a pre- and post-assessment tool.

Once the appropriate form and number of questions are determined and the pre-assessment administered, we recommend providing students feedback *without a grade* in order to best equip them with information

**Figure 3.5** Sample Assessment Questions: Aligned to RL.6.3, 6.5

*Sample does not include scoring guide/rubric.

**Surface-Level Questions (questions below the rigor of 6.3 and 6.5)**

1. Identify the setting of the story. Include the time period and location.
2. Identify the main character(s) of the story.
3. Recall and list 3 characteristics about the main character.
4. What was the theme of the text? Give 2 details from the book that helped you understand the theme.

**Midlevel Questions (questions at the rigor of 6.3 and 6.5)**

5. Describe the problem or conflict in the story. Name the problem and explain why it is an issue for the main character. Use 1 piece of evidence from the text in your answer. (RL.6.3)
6. Explain 2 events in the main character's life that led to the climax of the story and explain why, using 2 pieces of evidence from the text. (RL.6.3)
7. Explain which events led to a resolution of the problem in the story and explain why by citing 2 pieces of evidence from the text. (RL.6.3)
8. Explain how the main character changed over the course of the story. Cite 2 pieces of evidence from the text that support your answer. (RL.6.3)
9. How did the phrase, _____, affect how the main character responded? Explain your answer using 1 piece of evidence from the text. (RL.6.5)
10. Explain how Chapter ____ was significant in how the plot unfolded. Use 2 examples from Chapter ____ to support your answer. (RL.6.5)

**Deep Questions (questions that represent the next level of learning beyond 6.3 and 6.5)**

11. In class you had a chance to watch the movie that was based on the book. Explain 2 ways in which the screenplay was similar and 2 ways in which it was different from the book. (RL.6.7)
12. Explain how the resolution of the story is like a nonfiction text you have read in the past. Choose 1 text to compare to the story and give 2 examples of how they are similar. (RL.6.9)

needed to write personalized learning goals. The information must provide students with a deep understanding of what they know and don't know on the assessment, but also guard against students feeling like they have failed, are behind, or will be unable to achieve the Learning Intentions. The pre-assessment is *not a graded test;* rather, it is a *gauge* of prior knowledge. Teachers should mark answers as correct and incorrect, and offer specific feedback as to how the student may improve, what was missed, and so on. This gives students initial information about how they can reach the Learning Intentions and helps prepare them to write their own goals.

*Time for Application*

I. Revisiting an Assessment

We invite you to take a fresh look at an assessment you have developed in the past, or one that is from another source. Look carefully at each item and see if you can identify the standard or part of the standard being assessed and also determine the DOK level. Oftentimes, it is best to do this with a colleague or team, and to use the following questions to stimulate a conversation:

- Is each assessment item accurately aligned to the standard and the DOK?
- What is the balance between surface-level to deep-level questions?
- Is there an appropriate balance of surface-level to deep-level questions that are appropriate, given the time of year and expectations for students?
- What information will you be able to glean from each assessment item regarding your students' level of proficiency and their needs?
- How might the assessment provide students with information to be able to answer the following: *Where am I going? How am I doing? Where to next?*

II. Create Progress Checks

Use the information you have learned about surface to deep cognitive levels to create a one- or two-item progress check to administer during a unit of study. We encourage you to craft at least one assessment item that requires students to show their work when solving a problem or a written response. This will enable you to understand not only the students' understanding of a standard, but also the students' thinking processes rather than just a correct or incorrect response. Take time to generate a quick list of what must be included in the students' responses that will signal proficiency. This activity will prepare you for the process of constructing personalized learning goals and co-constructing Success Criteria, which will be discussed later in this chapter.

## 3. Use the Pre-assessment to Create Personalized Learning Goals

The act of having students write **personalized learning goals** is often misunderstood. We are not asking students to choose any goal under the sun. Instead, the idea is that students use the Learning Intentions, paired with their results from the pre-assessment, to establish focused and meaningful goals just for them. Our purpose is to ask students to be aware of which Learning Intentions they have already reached and which they need to learn more about in order to master the standards.

In *The Hidden Lives of Learners*, Graham Nuthall states, "Our research [of middle school students] has found that students already know, *on average*, about 50 percent of what a teacher intends his or her students to learn through a curriculum unit or topic. But that 50 percent is not evenly distributed. Different students know different things, and *all* of them will know only about 15 percent of what the teacher wants them to know" (Nuthall, 2007, pp. 35–36).

Hattie and Timperley (2007) explain that teachers can support students in goal-setting by (1) providing appropriate challenges; (2) pairing with specific goals, which will focus students' attention; and (3) aligning feedback to the specific goals through the use of clear criteria. They have discovered that these actions increase students' error-detection skills, commitment to reach their goals, and ability to develop self-regulation.

In order to put the research into action and take another step toward empowering students to become partners in learning, students need to ask and be able to answer these three critical questions:

1. *Where am I going?* or what are the Learning Intentions?

2. *How am I doing?* or which Learning Intentions do I already know and can demonstrate, and which am I still working to master?

3. *Where to next*? or what do I need to learn to close the gap to meet or exceed the standard?

Being able to ask and respond to these types of questions is a powerful part of partnering with students to share ownership of learning; however, many students may be unprepared to ask the questions, let alone answer them. Because this is not common practice in classrooms today, students will need modeling and support in order to write personalized learning goals. We suggest using a goal-setting graphic organizer or template that will offer them a way to compose and track their progress toward reaching their goals. The goal-setting graphic organizer can then be added to a personal learning portfolio that will include samples of student work that show growth and prove learning—ideas we will explore later in the book.

For now, let's review a few examples of goal-setting templates that can be used with students to support them in this process.

Goal-setting templates such as those provided can also be called "contracts" (Dean, Hubbell, Pitler, & Stone, 2012). They have been found to have positive effects on student ownership of learning because they afford students the ability to

- Have greater control over what they are learning
- Receive targeted instruction from the teacher
- Work in groups with others who have similar learning goals

- Focus on what matters most
- Better organize their time
- Give and receive feedback more effectively around personalized learning goals

**Figure 3.6** Example 1: Secondary Student Goals Template: Aligned to RL.6.3. 6.5

| **Name:** *Jamie, Grade 6* | **Class/Period:** *English Language Arts, Fourth Period* |
|---|---|
| **Learning Intentions Demonstrated on the Pretest** <br><br> • To explain how the plot moves a story along <br> • To describe how characters are affected by the events in the story <br> • To show how different parts of a story affect its meaning and the way the whole story turns out | **My Personal Learning Goals** <br><br> • I need to work on reading the text to better understand how the main character is affected by the events and how to explain that using examples from the story. <br> • I need to work on how different phrases and words the author uses have an effect on the plot. I get how events affect the plot but never really thought about how the words the author uses make a difference. |

**Figure 3.7** Example 2: Primary Student Goals Template (Do You Know Your A, B, Cs? ✓ indicates proficient)

| ✓ Aa | ✓ Bb | ✓ Cc | ☐ Dd |
|---|---|---|---|
| ☐ Ee | ☐ Ff | ✓ Gg | ✓ Hh |
| ☐ Ii | ☐ Jj | ✓ Kk | ✓ Ll |
| ☐ Mm | ☐ Nn | ✓ Oo | ✓ Pp |
| ☐ Qq | ✓ Rr | ✓ Ss | ✓ Tt |
| ✓ Uu | ✓ Vv | ✓ Ww | ✓ Xx |
| ✓ Yy | ✓ Zz | Name: | Logan |

## 4. Co-construct Success Criteria, Aligned to the Learning Intentions

*Learning objectives and Success Criteria are the tools which enable pupils to exercise power over their own learning.*

— Shirley Clarke, *Active Learning Through Formative Assessment*

Once students know *what* they need to learn, it is critical that we show them *how* to reach their goals. Providing the "how to" is what Success Criteria afford students. Margaret Heritage (2010) explains that Success Criteria identify what it takes to meet the learning goal and are used as checks on learning. Hattie (2012) states that there are two parts in targeted or focused learning: The first is being clear about what is to be learned from the lesson(s)—the Learning Intention; the second is having a way of knowing that the desired learning has been achieved—the Success Criteria. Figures 3.8 and 3.9 provide examples of Learning Intentions paired with

**Figure 3.8**  Learning Intentions and Success Criteria (Standard RL.6.3 and Standard RL.6.5)

| **Standard RL.6.3** | |
| --- | --- |
| DESCRIBE how a particular story's or drama's plot unfolds in a series of episodes. | DESCRIBE how the characters respond or change as the plot moves toward resolution. |
| **Corresponding Student-Friendly Learning Intentions** | |
| To explain how the plot moves a story along | To describe how characters are affected by the events in the story |
| **Success Criteria** | |
| • Describe how the time and setting in which a story takes place can affect the type of conflict or problem the main character(s) face.<br>• Connect the problem in the story to the events that led up to the climax.<br>• Show how the resolution ties up the story and resolves the problem or conflict for the main character(s). | • Connect the problem/conflict in the story to the resolution to show how the main character(s) changes.<br>• Show how other characters in the story interact during the events of the story and how their actions can affect the main character(s). |

| **Standard RL.6.5** |
| --- |
| ANALYZE how a particular sentence, chapter, scene, or stanza fits into the overall structure of a text and contributes to the development of the theme, setting, or plot. |
| **Corresponding Student-Friendly Learning Intentions** |
| To show how different parts of a story affect its meaning and the way the whole story turns out |
| **Success Criteria** |
| • Explain how the author uses word choice to shape the message in the story.<br>• Explain how each chapter relates to the others in order to move the plot along.<br>• Describe how the story would be different if particular scenes were missing from the text. |

**Figure 3.9** Additional Examples of Success Criteria Aligned to Learning Intentions

| Learning Goal or Intention | Success Criteria | Text |
|---|---|---|
| • Understand the structure of a coordinate grid | • To talk and write about accurately plotting points on a coordinate grid using correct vocabulary<br>• To accurately plot and label points in each quadrant on a coordinate grid | *Formative Assessment: Making It Happen in the Classroom* (2010) by Margaret Heritage, p. 46 |
| • To order stories | • We'll know we have achieved this because . . .<br>  ○ It will make sense<br>  ○ It will retell the story we heard | *Unlocking Formative Assessment: Practical Strategies for Enhancing Pupils' Learning in the Primary Classroom* (2001) by Shirley Clarke, p. 29 |
| • To know ways of controlling drought | • List the different causes of drought<br>• Explain how these could be reduced<br>• List your recommendations for how people can cope and live with drought<br>• Make comparisons with "drought" in the UK | *Formative Assessment in the Secondary Classroom* (2005) by Shirley Clarke, p. 33 |
| • We are learning to recognize sequence and to be able to write a series of events in order when it suits our purposes as writers. | • Our writing will begin with the very first thing that happened.<br>• Our writing will have all the events in the middle in the correct order of when things happened.<br>• Our writing will end with the very last thing that happened. | *Clarity in the Classroom: Using Formative Assessment for Building Learning-Focused Relationships* (2010) by Michael Absolum, pp. 84–85 |

Success Criteria. Take a few moments to review, and take particular notice of the relationship between the two.

Simple and clear Success Criteria are often missing from the classroom; further still from the classroom are **co-constructed Success Criteria**. Constructing the criteria for success enlists students to share in the process as partners to determine what it will take to accomplish the Learning Intentions. Shirley Clarke emphasized the importance of using Success

Criteria when she explained, "Using Success Criteria has had a major impact on both teaching and learning, but mainly in equipping pupils with the tools to be able to self- and peer-assess" (Clarke, 2008, p. 117).

How, then, can teachers learn to co-construct Success Criteria with students? We recommend teachers first conceptualize what criteria are needed to accomplish the Learning Intentions and then to work with students to co-construct the criteria in their words.

Starting with a deep understanding of the standards and a clear vision of proficiency will ensure that criteria critical to success will emerge during the co-construction process with students. Teachers must facilitate the conversation and ask appropriate questions that guide students to discover the appropriate criteria for success demanded by the standard(s). Below is a list of attributes Mary Jane O'Connell generated with teachers from Englewood School District in Colorado that provide insight into how to prepare to co-construct with students.

**Figure 3.10**   Conceptualizing Co-constructing Success Criteria

**What Teachers Need to Know**

1. Know the standard(s) deeply and the level of cognitive complexity embedded in the concepts and skills.

2. Understand the learning progressions to determine potential prerequisites and what is needed to accelerate learning.

3. Provide anonymous student work samples to show proficient work (exemplars) and, when appropriate or feasible, work that is not proficient to provide a comparison.

4. Be able to use multiple methods to co-construct Success Criteria with students.

5. Prepare questions or cues to help students discover the criteria for success.

6. Be able to transfer the Success Criteria to create a rubric, scoring guide, or checklist that minimizes subjective language.

7. Plan how to use the Success Criteria to formatively assess students.

8. Determine the best methods to provide effective feedback using the Success Criteria.

9. Model how to provide feedback to self or to peers using the Success Criteria (rubric, scoring guide, or checklist).

In *Active Learning Through Formative Assessment* (2008), Shirley Clarke discusses several effective techniques for co-constructing. The following co-constructing techniques have been adapted and expanded from Clarke's recommendations:

- Show students a finished piece of work from an anonymous peer. Ask them to work in pairs to first review the Learning Intention(s) and then to analyze the student work for how closely it aligns. Ask students to notice specific attributes or criteria in the sample and to record their ideas individually or in pairs. Next, ask students to share the attributes with the class to generate Success Criteria aligned to the Learning Intention(s).

- Provide students with two finished examples of anonymous student work—one example of high quality and the other of lesser quality. Ask students to compare the two pieces by first noticing the things that are the same to establish basic criteria. Next, ask them to look for things that are different to extend the criteria and explore the difference in quality of the two selections.

- Demonstrate a task; while doing so, ask students to identify what you are doing correctly to construct as you go along. Students can also be a part of the modeling of the task.

- Revise Success Criteria with students as they work through the learning process and discover additional criteria or decide that some criteria are unnecessary.

- Model a task, such as solving a math problem, leaving out many of the details. Then ask the students to explain how it should be done correctly. Collect their responses to establish initial criteria.

- Post or distribute the criteria for students to include in their learning portfolio. The Success Criteria should be revisited often and used to provide feedback.

- Revisit existing Success Criteria after a project or task is completed by asking students to reflect on what could be edited, removed, updated, or revised to better align to the Learning Intentions and to the quality of the product.

### *Time for Application*

I. Give It a Go

After carefully considering the information needed to begin the co-construction of Success Criteria, it is time to experiment and try several different approaches that have been used successfully by teachers. You can also create your own processes. You might consider reading one or two of the sources cited, or simply generate an Internet search for video clips of teachers engaging students in the process. Simply enter *Success Criteria* or *co-constructing criteria for success,* and you will be richly rewarded.

You will also find several links to videos we have found instructive in our work with teachers at www.corwin.com/partneringwithstudents.

## 5. Include Learner Beliefs as Part of the Criteria for Success

Now that expectations for learning are clear for students and teachers, it is critical that we add beliefs about learning to the conversation. Students can now answer three of the questions from the Learner's Internal Compass: *Where am I going? How am I doing? Where to next?* The final question is *How can I contribute?* In order to achieve the Handoff and fully empower students to be partners in learning, we need to establish which of the Learner Beliefs will best enable students to contribute to the learning that will take place in order that all students reach the Learning Intentions.

The following examples expand the student goals template to illustrate an important step: identifying personal Learner Beliefs. Given Jamie's grade level, it would be reasonable for her to generate Learner Beliefs independently (Figure 3.11). In the second example, a kindergarten student might be unable to categorize or select belief statements (Figure 3.12). The Learner Beliefs could therefore be stated to the student, written for the student or represented by images. To prepare students for this step, we suggest generating a list of Learner Beliefs by dividing students into partners or small groups before coming together to finalize a list for the whole group. If students have engaged in some of the suggested exercises in Chapter 1 and have created a Class Credo, this will be a natural next step. They should be able to identify their Learner Beliefs and begin to understand that these beliefs underpin their every action.

**Figure 3.11**  Secondary Student Goals Template (aligned to RL.6.3, 6.5)

| Name:<br>*Jamie, Grade 6* | Class/Period:<br>*English Language Arts, Fourth Period* |
|---|---|
| **Learning Intentions Demonstrated on the Pretest**<br><br>• To explain how the plot moves a story along<br>• To describe how characters are affected by the events in the story<br>• To show how different parts of a story affect its meaning and the way the whole story turns out | **My Personal Learning Goal**<br><br>• I need to work on reading the text to better understand how the main character is affected by the events and how to explain that using examples from the story.<br>• I need to work on how different phrases and words the author uses have an effect on the plot. I get how events affect the plot but never really thought about how the words the author uses make a difference. |

| Name:<br>*Jamie, Grade 6* | Class/Period:<br>*English Language Arts, Fourth Period* |
|---|---|
| **Success Criteria**<br><br>• Describe how the time and place can affect the type of conflict or problem the main character(s) face.<br>• Connect the problem in the story to the events that led up to the climax.<br>• Show how the resolution ties up the story and resolves the problem or conflict for the main character(s).<br>• Connect the problem/conflict in the story to the resolution to show how the main character(s) changes.<br>• Show how other characters in the story interact during the events of the story and how their actions can affect the main character(s).<br>• Explain how the author uses word choice to shape the message in the story.<br>• Explain how each chapter relates to the others in order to move the plot along.<br>• Describe how the story would be different if particular scenes were missing from the text. | **Beliefs That Will Support My Learning**<br><br>• I will ask for suggestions, help, and feedback to be sure I am reaching my learning goals.<br>• I will listen to others because I know we can learn from one another.<br>• I know that learning is hard work and that when I struggle through problems, I am becoming a better learner. |

**Figure 3.12** Primary Student Goals Template (Do You Know Your A, B, Cs? ✓ indicates proficient)

| ✓ Aa | ✓ Bb | ✓ Cc | ☐ Dd |
|---|---|---|---|
| ☐ Ee | ☐ Ff | ✓ Gg | ✓ Hh |
| ☐ Ii | ☐ Jj | ✓ Kk | ✓ Ll |
| ☐ Mm | ☐ Nn | ✓ Oo | ✓ Pp |
| ☐ Qq | ✓ Rr | ✓ Ss | ✓ Tt |
| ✓ Uu | ✓ Vv | ✓ Ww | ✓ Xx |
| ✓ Yy | ✓ Zz | Name: | Logan |

| **Success Criteria** | **Beliefs** |
|---|---|
| • I can focus on the letters I don't yet know. | • I believe that practicing every day will help me learn all my letters. |

*(Continued)*

**Figure 3.12** (Continued)

| Success Criteria | Beliefs |
|---|---|
| • I can tell the difference between upper- and lowercase letters.<br>• I can practice writing and saying my letters.<br>• I can practice finding the letters in a story. | • I will try and try again until I get them all.<br>• I know that friends can help me practice and they have different letters to learn than I do. |

### Fifth-Grade Personal Narrative Goal-Setting Sample

To view another goal-setting template created with input from fifth-grade students studying personal narrative, see Appendix H. The sample was provided by Tara Lindburg of Academy Charter School in Castle Rock, Colorado, and incorporates the mind frames or Learner Beliefs that will help build their talent for learning as part of the Success Criteria for the unit of study. The template includes the standard, the co-constructed Success Criteria, and the mind frames or beliefs that will be necessary for students to achieve the task.

### Time for Application

I. Class Credo and Nonacademic Success Criteria

If you have not generated a Class Credo to capture Learner Beliefs, you might be inspired to revisit Chapter 1 and give it a try with your students. Even if you haven't co-constructed academic Success Criteria, think about co-constructing Success Criteria around classroom expectations for independent work, homework completion, group work, classroom discussion, proper etiquette for a school-wide assembly, and so on. Next, identify the Learner Beliefs from the Class Credo. If you have not developed a Class Credo, ask questions such as *Why are these criteria or expectations needed in our classroom or school? How does it help you and others?* This exercise will also enable students to begin developing the cardinal point, north, on the Learner's Internal Compass: *What is my contribution?*

II. Getting Goal-Directed

Adapt or create your own goal-setting template with colleagues, or be adventurous and involve the students in the process to generate greater investment. You might consider sharing the template from the book as a starting point for students to critique and revise. It is available at www.corwin.com/partneringwithstudents.

The goal-setting template should continue to evolve to meet the students' needs. The template provides the information needed to offer feedback and help students answer all the questions on the Learner's Internal Compass.

## SUMMING UP: DEFINING CRITERIA FOR SUCCESS

Throughout the chapter, we have provided a step-by-step approach to empowering students to set the course for learning. Just as the teacher needs clarity regarding what is to be learned and how to determine the criteria for success, students also need this information to set meaningful goals. As a result, students will be able to answer the questions *Where am I going? How am I doing? Where to next?* and *What is my contribution?* The Learner's Internal Compass is now aligned and primed for the learning to take place.

**Teacher's Internal Compass**

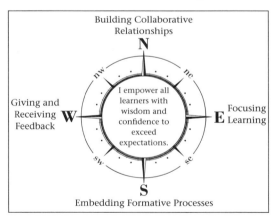

**Learner's Internal Compass**

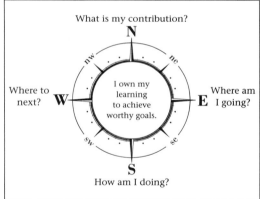

As we wrap up Chapter 3, reflect on the deliberate practices and beliefs that both teachers and students must employ. Which do you think have been launched and will be further explored during learning and after it has taken place?

Use the next steps template to reflect on and plan how you will implement one to three actions, and what you expect from your students as you begin to define the criteria for success.

## Next Steps: A Template for Reflection and Planning

*How can teachers translate standards into criteria for success?*

*How can students develop personalized learning goals?*

*How do we put beliefs about learning into action?*

| Teacher's Role | Student's Role |
|---|---|
| Defining the Journey: | Defining the Journey: |

For resources related to defining criteria for success, go to www.corwin .com/partneringwithstudents.

# Part II

# Learning on the Journey

# 4 Learner Strategies for Life

*How do teachers support students in developing strategies for learning?*

———————————— ❧ ❧ ❧ ❧ ————————————

*Learning is about one's relationship with oneself and one's ability to exert the effort, self-control, and critical self-assessment necessary to achieve the best possible results—and about overcoming risk aversion, failure, distraction, and sheer laziness in pursuit of real achievement. This is self-regulated learning.*

—Linda Nilson, *Creating Self-Regulated Learners: Strategies to Strengthen Students' Self-Awareness and Learning Skills*

As teachers, we plan our lessons for students to absorb the content—yet how often have we heard or voiced ourselves, "I taught it yesterday, but today they acted like they have never heard it before in their lives. Why don't they remember what I teach them?" While it is a complaint that will probably be voiced in the hallways, teachers' lounges, and classrooms of schools for years to come, it is not one that has the potential to change our practice or outcomes for learners. *The question is not about teaching; it is about learning.* The question is: "Did my students learn it?" As teachers, we can stand on our heads, give the most riveting lectures, teach like our hair is on fire, but the question remains the same: "Did all my effort as a teacher result in learning for my students?" *Instead of focusing on what was taught, the focus should be on what was learned.*

In an interview, John Hattie reflected upon a question he often poses to teachers participating in professional development:

> "What learning theories are you using?" The answer is often a long silence. You'll hear a lot about teaching methods but notions about learning are missing. And so constantly focusing on how students are learning, what they're learning, and what their progress is— that's what I want us to pay attention to. I want us to get away from the debates we have about teaching. (Zegarac, 2013)

Currently, a wealth of knowledge exists in the marketplace offering educators almost endless resources that describe mountains of teaching strategies to better instruction. As educators ourselves, we welcome these resources that encourage the use of many highly effective instructional strategies. However, the issue lies with the *ownership of the strategies*. When the teacher is the owner of the strategy and the focus is on delivering the content, we sell our learners short. *The more important half of the learning equation is to teach students to be more skillful at learning and be able to surface the actions that led to their success.* Students can both learn the content and gain insight into Learner Strategies for the future, which is a win–win situation. In *High Impact Instruction*, Knight adds that teaching students *how* to learn is likely at least as important as teaching students *what* to learn (2013).

Our goal is to empower students to build a *personal toolbox of learning strategies* that they can apply to new learning situations throughout a lifetime, thus reaching True North. When students own their learning and set ambitious goals, the path initially may be unclear. However, a few roadblocks will not daunt students who have developed a resolute mindset intent on success. They will consult their toolbox of strategies or actively research alternative solutions and resources to learn and ultimately succeed. In other words, students with a personal toolbox of learning strategies know what to do when they "get stuck." They know how to seek help, detect errors, ask questions, access resources, and explore possibilities. These are skills for a lifetime of learning. "Only lifelong learners will be able to keep up with the explosive growth of knowledge and skills in their career and to retool into a new career after their previous one runs its course" (Nilson, 2013, p. 1). Each point of the compass for both the teacher and the learner is at work during the teaching and learning process. Take a few moments to reflect on each cardinal point and to make connections about how each is critical to the learning process.

**Teacher's Internal Compass**

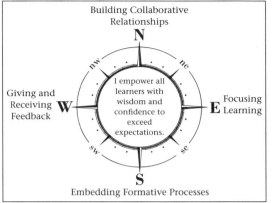

**Learner's Internal Compass**

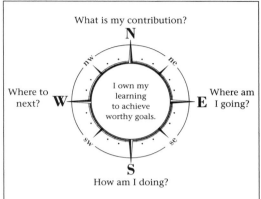

# LAYING THE FOUNDATION FOR LEARNER STRATEGIES

According to the Oxford Dictionaries (2014), strategies are "a plan of action designed to achieve a long-term or overall aim." In this model, we encourage teachers to have a two-fold aim related to the use of strategies:

- Students learn the necessary concepts and skills to master the content.
- Students learn strategies that they can apply to achieve worthy goals throughout their lives.

Another way to think about strategies that aligns with our two-fold purpose is to think of the closely related word, *strategic*. How can we as teachers be *most* strategic? How can students be *most* strategic? We know that students will face challenges and innovations that have yet to be dreamt of, and we need to prepare them to be ready for learning far beyond the content provided during their formal education.

We have all experienced learners in our classroom who work hard, pick things up quickly, and seem to be good at learning in every content area. Learners like these own or possess a toolbox of strategies that can be applied to many situations, enabling them to progress through the learning process with efficiency and confidence. For example, think of your strongest reader. Is it that you taught that student every reading skill and strategy more effectively than you did the others? Most likely not. There is a greater chance that the student is unconsciously metacognitive and has through trial and error engaged in mental questioning and observations. The student has adopted skills and strategies that have become internalized. As a result, the student has developed an extensive repertoire of reading skills that have become part of his or her own reading toolbox.

Studies by Bandura (1977, 1997) have found that the beliefs students hold about their own self-efficacy determines how capable they feel as self-regulated learners. In turn, those students with greater self-efficacy and self-regulation skills learn more, which also proves to further boost their confidence as learners (Nilson, 2013). To further define this idea, the following definitions from Bandura have been provided.

| | |
|---|---|
| **Perceived self-efficacy:** People's beliefs about their capabilities to produce desired effects. | **Self-regulation:** Exercise of influence over one's own motivation, thought processes, emotional states, and patterns of behavior. |

*Source:* "Self-Efficacy," by A. Bandura, 1994. In V. S. Ramachaudran (Ed.), *Encyclopedia of Human Behavior* (Vol. 4, pp. 71–81). New York: Academic Press.

On the other hand, we also know the students in our classroom who don't believe they are good learners and exhibit characteristics of a fixed mindset. These students often lack both confidence and strategies for learning, and many times they struggle to explain their own thinking and process skills. A common issue that arises when teaching such students is motivation. When motivation is perceived to be the cause for lack of performance, it can be fairly common to blame the teacher, the student, and sometimes even the parent (Wiliam, 2011). You might hear comments such as, "That kid just doesn't care. She never turns in any homework, and her parents are too busy. The teacher hasn't even bothered to call home." Our job is to change our practices, and as a result to alter students' mindsets and equip them with strategies that will boost their learning as well as the opportunities for their future.

In 1990, Mihaly Csikszentmihalyi explored the issues related to motivation in his book *Flow: The Psychology of Optimal Experience*. He discovered a deeper and more relevant issue that relates to motivation. If the learning task is too easy and there is little challenge, there will be little motivation even to attempt the task or exert much effort. How many times do we "dummy down" the work and deny our struggling learners a meaningful challenge worth the effort? Is it any wonder that these students are unmotivated? Conversely, if we set the bar too high and offer a challenge without teaching the necessary skills or providing the appropriate scaffolding, our learners will mask their fears and anxieties and will fail to engage. Sometimes these students are labeled as unmotivated or lazy.

However, if the task is appropriately challenging and matched to the level of the learner, motivation is increased. Csikszentmihalyi maintains there is a "flow" between challenging learning tasks and the development of Learner Strategies that leads to increased content knowledge. When students are fully absorbed in the learning, not only is their motivation heightened, but their capacity to learn is stretched.

Figure 4.1 depicts the relationship between the level of challenge, the capacity of the learner, and the subsequent level of motivation. First, review the equation and then the relationships between challenge and capacity to explore how each factor relates to motivation.

**Figure 4.1** Level of Challenge + Level of Capacity of Learner = Level of Motivation

| Level of Challenge | Level of Capacity of Learner | Level of Motivation |
|---|---|---|
| Low | Low | Apathy—lack of challenge |
| High | Low | Anxiety—fear of failure |
| High | High | "Flow"—high motivation |

## DEFINING LEARNER STRATEGIES

At this point you may be asking, *What types of strategies will empower students?*

To put it simply, **Learner Strategies** are the strategies or actions that will accelerate learning forward and can be applied to future learning experiences. In Figure 4.2 (following), we have listed some examples. As you read through this figure you may notice that many of the examples align with strategies that skillful teachers use in the classroom. However, our premise is that some students are able to see how to use and apply these strategies on their own, while many students fail to make a Transfer between a teacher-owned strategy and the idea that they could use the same strategy for their own learning. *Our goal is to increase students' awareness of the strategies, empower them as strategic partners in learning, and equip them for future endeavors.* But this Transfer does not happen for all students unless we *intentionally* make it part of the learning process.

**Figure 4.2**   Examples of Learner Strategies

- Setting personal learning goals
- Assessing prior knowledge
- Planning strategies to tackle a task
- Organizing information
- Problem-solving
- Note-taking
- Self-teaching
- Modeling Reciprocal teaching
- Nonlinguistic representations
- Summarizing learning
- Metacognition/Reflection of learning
- Discussion strategies
- Collaboration skills
- Research strategies
- Help-seeking
- Leadership skills
- Self-assessment of learning and strategies

### *Time for Application*

I. Surfacing Learner Strategies

After reviewing the examples of Learner Strategies, reflect on how many you use in the classroom regularly. You might think about strategies unique to a discipline such as Mathematical Practices outlined in the Common Core Standards or perhaps specific strategies related to becoming a proficient reader. Consider strategies used in science, athletics, the arts, and so on.

- Can you think of any Learner Strategies you have witnessed your students using that aren't on the list and could be added?
- What strategies do your *students* employ independently to help them learn?

## THE TRANSFER OF LEARNER STRATEGIES

With strategies in mind, it is critical to discuss the way in which we transfer the strategies from teacher-owned to student-owned. Let's begin by discussing the idea of *Transfer.*

**Transfer** refers to students adopting strategies for learning from what is modeled in the classroom to their own toolbox for learning. It is important to explain, however, that not all strategies are meant to fully transfer to students, while others are.

Think of a strategy such as cooperative learning. The teacher may use a particular structure, such as Rallyrobin from Kagan's book *Cooperative Learning* (1994), where students work in pairs, taking turns to solve and coach each step of a problem. While students will learn some valuable discussion and interpersonal skills from the experience, they are unlikely to organize a Rallyrobin structure when engaging in a discussion with a study group or talking with friends. However, the experience is still highly valuable in reaching the Learning Intention and in gaining strategies to partner with other learners. We call this **Partial Transfer.**

**Full Transfer,** on the other hand, is possible when students can fully embrace and use a strategy in the future. An example of this type of a strategy is note-taking. A teacher may model how to use a concept map, Cornell notes, or key word notes. With each form of note-taking, students may fully adopt the various formats as Learner Strategies for future use.

Achieving Transfer, whether full or partial, is our goal in partnering with students to build ownership of learning. We consider the Transfer of strategies a multistep process that aligns with the learning process beautifully. Before instruction occurs, we recommend that teachers think through three considerations related to transferring strategies from teacher-owned to student-owned:

1. Review the Learning Intentions and the performance on the pre-assessment.

   o What instructional strategies would best support students in reaching the Learning Intention(s)?
   o What evidence from the pre-assessment can inform the types of strategies that students could use to reach the Learning Intention(s)?

2. Reflect on the types of Learner Strategies students already possess and use regularly.

   o What Learner Strategies have I witnessed my students using in the past?
   o When do I see my students able to work independently? What strategies do they employ during those times?
   o Do I have any students who may be able to teach a Learner Strategy to others? (aligns to *What is my contribution?*)

3. Determine the types of Learner Strategies to be shared with students during each phase of the teaching and learning process (before, during, and after).

   o Which strategies might best support my students before we begin new learning, or might be at the surface level of the learning progression? (aligns to *Where am I going?*)
   o Which strategies would best support students while we learn or as we move from surface to deep learning? (aligns to *How am I doing?*)
   o Which strategies would best support my students as we begin to summarize, reflect, and assess learning to determine *Where to next?*

In Figure 4.3, you will notice that we have grouped Learner Strategies as they align to the time frames within the learning process. Take a moment to notice that different Learner Strategies can be used more than once, and when it is best to use a strategy during a particular time frame or phase.

**Figure 4.3** Examples of Learner Strategies Aligned to the Learning Process

| **BEFORE** | • Setting personal learning goals<br>• Assessing prior knowledge<br>• Planning strategies to tackle a task |
| --- | --- |
| **DURING** | • Organizing information<br>• Problem-solving<br>• Note-taking<br>• Self-teaching<br>• Modeling<br>• Reciprocal teaching<br>• Summarizing learning<br>• Metacognition/Reflection of learning<br>• Discussion strategies<br>• Collaboration skills<br>• Research strategies<br>• Help-seeking<br>• Leadership skills<br>• Self-assessment of learning and strategies<br>• Giving and receiving feedback |
| **AFTER** | • Summarizing learning<br>• Metacognition Reflection of learning<br>• Discussion strategies<br>• Self-assessment of learning and strategies |

Once a teacher has selected a number of Learner Strategies to include in an upcoming unit of study or a chunk of instruction, it is necessary to think about what it will take for the Transfer to occur to ensure that students own the strategy. As previously mentioned, some students will naturally transfer effective or meaningful strategies into their own toolbox, while others will struggle to do so. We propose that certain actions—both thinking and doing—must take place in order for Transfer to occur for all students. These actions include but are not limited to modeling, metacognition, choice, monitoring and reflection, revision, and the ability to use the strategy independently. Figure 4.4 provides a definition of each action a teacher might consider to transfer strategies to students.

**Figure 4.4**   Six Actions to Transfer Teacher-Owned to Learner-Owned Strategies

| Action | Explanation |
|---|---|
| **Modeling** | Explicit demonstration of one's thinking and doing so that others may replicate the same actions |
| **Metacognition** | Thinking about one's own thinking; processing bridge between teacher-owned and student-owned strategies |
| **Choice** | Knowing and being able to select a strategy that will best meet the needs or preferences of a learner |
| **Monitoring and reflection** | Conscious appraisal of whether or not a strategy is having the desired effect during and after learning |
| **Revision of strategy** | Modification of a strategy in order to provide greater learning. How could the strategy change or be combined with another to get a better result? |
| **Independent use** | Application of a strategy to other learning experiences. Is this a strategy that can be used independently or for a personal purpose? |

The following provides an example of the six actions used to support students in making the Transfer from a teacher-owned strategy to a student-owned strategy. Suppose that in a unit of study a teacher felt it necessary for students to take notes from several different texts. The students must be able to accurately record meaningful information from each text, and to organize, process, and remember specific information about a topic. In doing so, the teacher felt it necessary to share several forms of note-taking with his students and designed the following instructional sequence:

- On three separate days, the teacher selected one note-taking method to share with the students. He modeled Cornell notes, a concept map, and an outline for his students each day. After the modeling, students were asked to try each form of note-taking, using a different text from the same genre. (Modeling)
- After students tried each form of note-taking, he again asked them to think about how that form of note-taking helped them organize and process information about the topic. Students shared their ideas in small groups and then as a class. (Metacognition)
- Once students felt comfortable with each type of note-taking, the teacher presented them with a new text to read and digest. She asked each student to skim the text and determine which type of note-taking he or she would personally find most effective to use. (Choice)
- As each student worked through the text, taking notes in his or her chosen format, the teacher stopped the class to ask how the format for note-taking was working. Students were allowed to modify and change their format if they were finding it difficult to use the format they initially selected. (Monitoring and Reflection + Revision of Strategy)
- Once students had completed the task, he asked them to discuss which type of note-taking worked best, and why. He then asked students to develop a list of criteria for which types of text and purposes best fit each type of note-taking. (Independent Use)
- The teacher also recorded observations on the type of note-taking formats the students used independently, and with which types of text. She shared this information with the students to stimulate a class discussion on choice and individual preferences as well as how to best modify strategies to optimize effectiveness. (Monitoring and Reflection + Revision of Strategy + Independent Use)

In this scenario, the teacher used each of the six actions to ensure that students made the Transfer to the ownership of note-taking that can be accessed by students in various learning situations. In future learning experiences, he might continue to allow choice as well as sharing new formats such as key word notes, list-making, drawing word-pictures, and more. Over time, students will become better prepared to select the most effective way to take notes for their personal learning needs as they encounter more challenging content.

This might sound like a nice idea in theory, but many readers may wonder if it is really worth their time to equip students with Learner Strategies around note-taking. Interestingly, a great deal of research has been done to highlight the benefit of explicit teaching on multiple note-taking formats

(Dean, Hubbell, Pitler, & Stone, 2012). "Very few students are taught even basic 'note-taking' skills . . . despite the fact that students are expected to take extensive notes . . . and despite the recognized usefulness of note taking for storing, learning, and thinking about what is being taught" (Boch & Piolat, 2005 p. 79).

Granted, your topic or unit of study may have different needs for Learner Strategies; therefore, we recommend using the six actions to Transfer the strategy you plan to use in the classroom from teacher-owned to learner-owned.

### Time for Application

I. Transferring Teacher-Owned Strategies

Take a moment to use the chart below in Figure 4.5 and insert your own strategy, thinking through how each action might be used to make the Transfer.

**Figure 4.5** Transferring Teacher-Owned Strategies Utilizing the Six Actions

| Action | My Strategy |
|---|---|
| **Modeling** | |
| **Metacognition** | |
| **Choice** | |
| **Monitoring and reflection** | |
| **Revision of strategy** | |
| **Independent use** | |

II. Partnering to Ensure Transfer

Consider partnering with colleagues to work through the six actions. You might agree to observe one another or create a video of one or more of the six actions for the purpose of sharing experiences and refining the process. You may want to discuss the reactions of students as you share feedback that acknowledges what worked and how to make the Transfer of learning even more effective.

Asking students to partner with you may be another terrific way to begin the process. Let the students know that the strategies you are teaching will provide various methods about *how to learn* now and in the future. Be sure to emphasize that mastering a Learner Strategy involves not only practice, reflection, revision, and a personal choice, but also knowing *when* to use a particular strategy to achieve a desired outcome.

# BUILDING A PORTFOLIO OF LEARNING

To further transfer and connect *what is being learned* to the *strategies being used to learn*, we recommend building a **learning portfolio** with students. The idea of the portfolio is not new. However, the connectedness of this portfolio is meant to empower students to be owners of their learning, and also to facilitate partnering with others in learning. By developing a learning portfolio, the goal is to inform students of the amazing strides they have made in learning, while simultaneously asking them to reflect on what empowered them to reach their goals. We will further define how this portfolio can be used to prove learning in Chapter 6. For now, as teachers and students work through a unit of study or a chunk of learning, we recommend collecting artifacts and using Learning Maps (Knight, 2013) to begin building the learning portfolio. The artifacts and Learning Maps will empower students to process and make connections about their learning, and later help them prove what they learned and how they learned it. In other words, a distinguishing addition to the typical portfolio is the inclusion of a critical element: *documenting Learner Strategies that are connected to the evidence of learning*. We will briefly describe first the types of artifacts to collect during the learning, and then how to use Learning Maps to process and connect learning.

## Artifacts

The learning portfolio is designed to be a living document to which students add over time. It is designed not to be a representation of the end of learning, but of the journey of learning. Artifacts should include the student goals template, Learning Maps, work samples, homework, rough drafts, pre-assessments, journal entries, and any other representations of student understanding, knowledge, skills, and questions about learning. Tied to these forms of evidence, students should also include information about the strategies they have used as learners. For example, if a homework assignment included gathering research from two different sources, students may include the note-taking strategies they employed when gathering the information. As students begin to catalog the Learner Strategies they used, each student's toolbox of strategies grows, as does the student's ability to take on new learning challenges. Students who consciously evaluate the usefulness of learning strategies and adopt those that work best into their practice as learners achieve Partial or Full Transfer of strategies.

Explanation and examples of what a student may collect in his or her learning portfolio appear in Figures 4.6, 4.7 and 4.8. Figure 4.6 explains what should be included in the learning portfolio thus far. Figure 4.7 provides a description of Learning Maps, and Figure 4.8 is a sample of a student-generated Learning Map. As you read ahead to learn more about Learning Maps, be conscious of the example provided of what a student may collect to archive in his or her learning portfolio.

As we dive into feedback in Chapter 5 and proving learning in Chapter 6, we will continue to use the portfolio as a powerful way to make learning visible and to reveal the remaining sections (4 and 5) of the learning portfolio.

**Figure 4.6**   Artifacts for the Learning Portfolio

| 1 | 2 | 3 | 4 | 5 |
|---|---|---|---|---|
| Student goals template (including the Learning Intentions, Success Criteria, and personalized learning goals) | Learning Maps, work samples, homework, practice, photos, rough drafts, pre-assessment, etc. | Learner Strategies aligned to artifacts collected | | |

## Learning Maps

In *High-Impact Instruction: A Framework for Great Teaching* (2013), Jim Knight explains how Learning Maps highlight the knowledge, skills, and big ideas that students should learn during a lesson, unit, or course. **Learning Maps** offer students a visual or graphic organizer, similar to a concept map, to depict the Learning Intentions. They can help students conceptually organize, visualize, and anticipate *Where am I going?* and also provide teachers and students a vehicle to surface *How am I doing?* and *Where to next?* Therefore, Learning Maps provide students a concrete Learner Strategy to frame and organize their learning as they progress through the learning process. In the portfolio, the Learning Map may serve as an artifact to document what has been learned while also cataloging the learning strategies employed. They provide students a processing tool for learning, which Knight describes as a "living study guide."

**Figure 4.7** Defining Learning Maps

Chapter 4:
Learning Maps

— is about →

creating graphic organizers depicting knowledge, skills, and big ideas

by defining → learning map
- Starting map
- Final map

by understanding → why they are used
- Keep students and teachers on track
- Show the big picture
- Structure the beginning and end of lesson
- Review
- Make connecting explicit
- Help struggling note-takers
- Are a living study guide

by comparing → types of maps
- Mind maps
- Concept maps
- Thinking maps
- Concept structures

by knowing → the parts of a learning map
- Core idea
- Subtopic
- Detail
- Lines
- Line label

by knowing → how to create maps
- Collect everything.
- Lay it out.
- Organize.
- Simplify.

by creating → quality learning maps
- Consider your legacy.
- Keep your map simple.
- Use line labels.
- Organize in the sequence of learning.
- Answer all the questions.

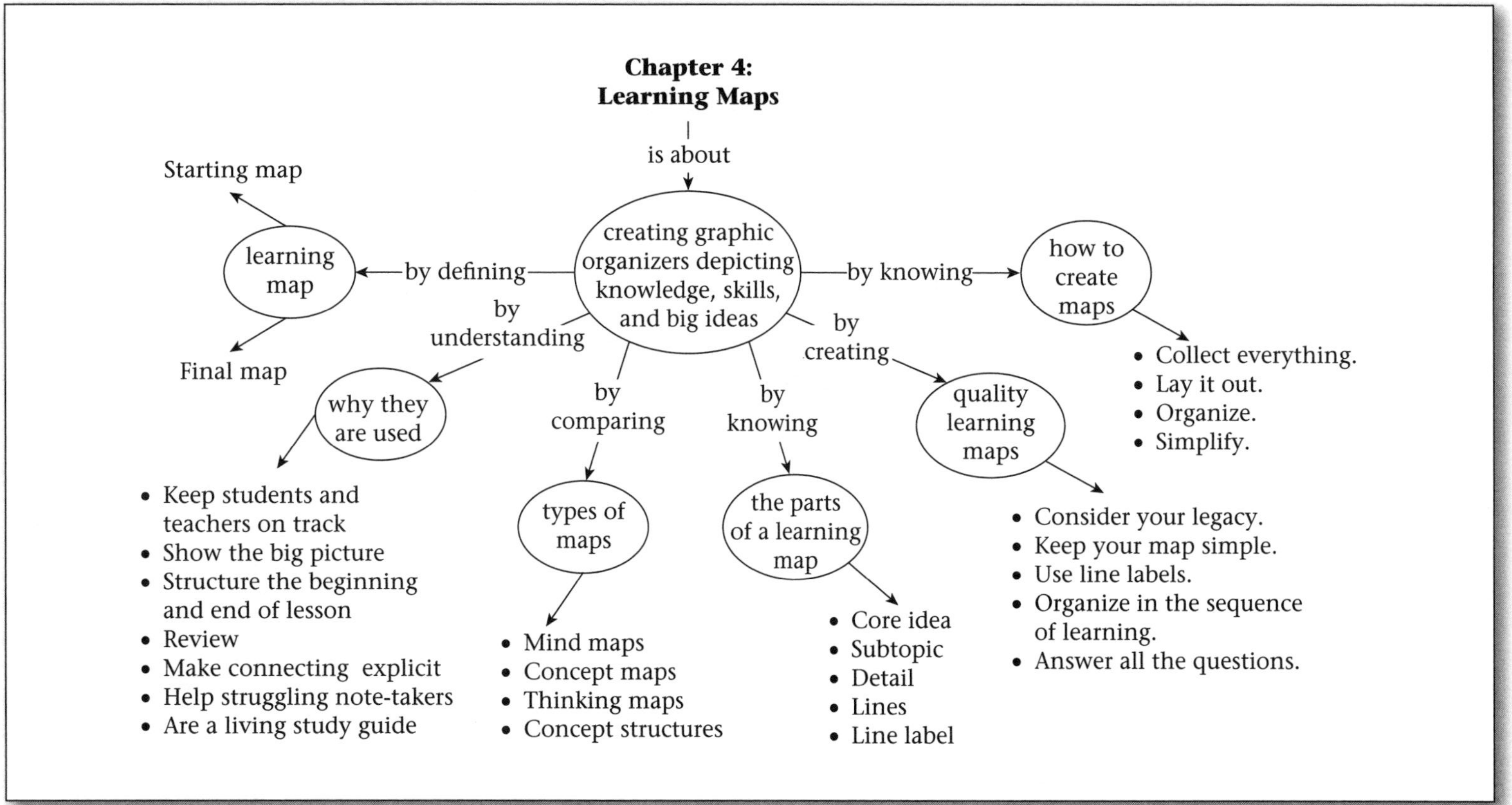

*Source: High-Impact Instruction: A Framework for Great Teaching, by J. Knight, 2013, p. 86. Thousand Oaks, CA: Corwin.*

**Figure 4.8** Middle School Student Example of a Science Learning Map

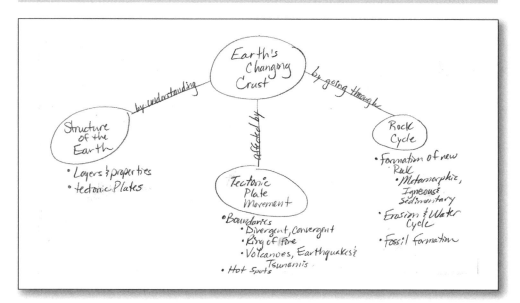

In Figure 4.7, you will find a Learning Map created by Jim Baxter, the 2014 Kansas Teacher of the Year. It provides a visual representation of the essential characteristics of Learning Maps and the benefits for students. Take a moment to review the examples in Figures 4.7 and 4.8 and reflect on how including a Learning Map in the portfolio may further student learning.

The Learning Map may be included as a living, breathing part of the portfolio; it should begin with the most important ideas from a unit or chunk of learning, derived from the standards and Learning Intentions. When introducing a new unit of study, the teacher identifies essential learning for the unit, which might also include topics and subtopics. As the unit progresses, the teacher and students revisit the Learning Maps regularly to record their growing understanding of the concepts and topics. The map will allow students time to connect ideas and break topics and subtopics into smaller parts, thus building a visual representation of their learning.

### Time for Application

I. Adding Learner Strategies

Let's return to Jamie's example, first presented in Chapter 3, to engage you in thinking about Learner Strategies the sixth-grader might use and potential artifacts she could collect.

In Figure 4.9, a space is provided to identify several Learner Strategies you might suggest or help Jamie develop. If needed, refer to the Learner Strategies listed in Figure 4.2.

**Figure 4.9**  Applying Learner Strategies and Collecting Artifacts

| Name:<br>*Jamie, Grade six* | Class/Period:<br>*English Language Arts, Fourth Period* |
|---|---|
| **Learning Intentions Demonstrated on the Pretest**<br><br>• To explain how the plot moves a story along<br>• To describe how characters are affected by the events in the story<br>• To show how different parts of a story affect its meaning and the way the whole story turns out | **My Personal Learning Goals**<br><br>• I need to work on reading the text to better understand how the main character is affected by the events and how to explain that using examples from the story.<br>• I need to work on how different phrases and words the author uses have an effect on the plot. I get how events affect the plot but never really thought about how the words the author uses make a difference. |
| **Success Criteria**<br><br>• Describe how the time and place can affect the type of conflict or problem the main character(s) face.<br>• Connect the problem in the story to the events that led up to the climax.<br>• Show how the resolution ties up the story and resolves the problem or conflict for the main character(s).<br>• Connect the problem/conflict in the story to the resolution to show how the main character(s) changes.<br>• Show how other characters in the story interact during the events of the story and how their actions can affect the main character(s).<br>• Explain how the author uses word choice to shape the message in the story.<br>• Explain how each chapter relates to the others in order to move the plot along.<br>• Describe how the story would be different if particular scenes were missing from the text. | **Beliefs That Will Support My Learning**<br><br>• I will ask for suggestions and feedback to be sure I am reaching my learning goals.<br>• I will listen to others because I know we can learn from one another.<br>• I know that learning is hard work, and that when I struggle through problems I am becoming a better learner.<br><br>**Learner Strategies** (see Figure 4.2) |

# SUMMING UP: LEARNER STRATEGIES FOR LIFE

The foundation has been laid and the supporting structures are under construction to initiate students into the process of owning learning. The transferring of teacher-owned strategies to student-owned strategies and embracing the responsibility for learning is a critical step in building independence in students.

At this point, you may be thinking that this all seems like a lot of steps, reflection time, and thinking in order to partner with students—and to be sure, it is. However, just as you will be working to move students to greater self-efficacy and self-regulation, you will also begin to move in the same direction when employing the ideas, strategies, and concepts shared in this book. Over time, it will become a part of what you do naturally, and you will continue to deepen your own practice as you go. The process of partnering with students is designed to follow the natural teaching and learning cycle and to enhance, deepen, and better inform and empower learners.

Use the next steps template to reflect on and plan how you will implement one to three actions, and what you expect from your students as you begin to consider the strategies that can promote their learning for life.

## Next Steps: A Template for Reflection and Planning

*How do teachers support students in developing strategies for learning?*

| Teacher's Role | Student's Role |
| --- | --- |
| Learning on the Journey: | Learning on the Journey: |

# 5 Learning Through Effective Feedback

*How can feedback propel learning forward for teachers and students?*

———— ✖ ✖ ✖ ✖ ————

*Our fundamental role is to constantly evaluate the impact we have on kids. We must be willing to be exposed based on evidence; we must have the conversations. We are change agents.*

—John Hattie, keynote address, 90/90/90 Schools
Summit, Leadership and Learning Center, 2011

**D**o you believe you are a change agent? Do you believe you have the power to change learning and the future for your students? These powerful ideas, while seemingly idealistic, are at the heart of effective feedback.

We know that students receive a great deal of feedback every day, as do teachers. In fact, according to Stone and Heen (2014), students receive over three hundred assignments, papers, and tests back from their teachers each year. We also know that feedback has the potential to double the speed of learning (Wiliam, 2011). However, the issue remains that many students still aren't achieving the Learning Intentions, let alone reaching or exceeding grade-level proficiency standards. A great divide exists between what we know to be effective and what is actually transpiring in the classroom when feedback is considered.

When we break the word *feedback* down to its parts, we find the words *feed*, meaning to nourish, and *back*, meaning "in return" or "in exchange." Therefore, **feedback** *is meant to nourish learning through an exchange.* As teachers, we must ask ourselves, "Is feedback in my classroom nourishing learning for both myself and the students?"

In *Feedback: The Hinge That Joins Teaching and Learning*, Pollock (2012, p. 5) states, "Considering feedback as a learning strategy, not just something teachers are required to do, inspires teachers to teach students to self-evaluate and use feedback from others as a critical part of all lessons." In the previous chapter, we explored the idea of Learner Strategies as critical tools for empowering students to become partners in learning. Feedback is an essential part of the learning process and one of the most critical Learner Strategies, which is why an entire chapter is devoted to its practice. As change agents, we have the power to make the learning experience in the classroom what we hope and dream for our students and ourselves.

You will notice that on the Teacher's Internal Compass we are rotating our attention to the cardinal points *South: Embedded Formative Assessments and West: Giving and Receiving Feedback*, which enables teachers to receive direct feedback on how their instruction is moving learning forward and whether to stay the course, adjust, or completely revamp instruction. Teachers use information gleaned from a variety of formative assessments to tailor the type of feedback needed to nourish and propel learning forward.

In the classroom, students are also learning how to receive and act upon feedback from three sources: the teacher, other students, and the self. Students must learn how to give feedback that is accurate and delivered appropriately to their teachers and other students. When teachers and students partner to own the learning process, they have an unquenchable thirst for feedback that answers the questions *Where am I going? How am I doing?* and *Where to next?*

The Learner's Internal Compass fluctuates between the cardinal points East, South, and West, depending on where the learner is in the teaching and learning cycle. In *Thanks for the Feedback* (2014), Stone and Heen conclude that "creating pull" is the leverage used to manage and learn from all types of feedback. "Creating pull is about mastering the skills required to drive our own learning; it's about how to engage in feedback conversations with confidence and curiosity, and even when the feedback is wrong, how to find insight that might help us grow" (Stone & Heen, 2014, p. 6).

**Teacher's Internal Compass**

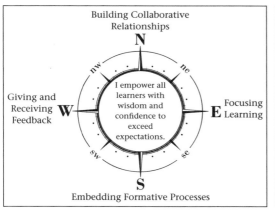

Building Collaborative Relationships

N

Giving and Receiving Feedback

W

I empower all learners with wisdom and confidence to exceed expectations.

E Focusing Learning

S

Embedding Formative Processes

**Learner's Internal Compass**

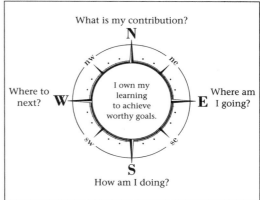

What is my contribution?

N

Where to next?

W

I own my learning to achieve worthy goals.

E Where am I going?

S

How am I doing?

# NOURISHING LEARNING THROUGH FEEDBACK

> The major message seems to be that students—regardless of achievement level—prefer teachers to provide more feedback that is forward-looking, related to the success of the lesson, and "just in time" and "just for me" (and not "about me").
>
> —John Hattie, *Visible Learning for Teachers: Maximizing Impact on Teachers*

It is important to point out that students will often lead us to better practices provided we observe carefully, ask for feedback, listen, and respond in a timely manner. When asked about what works and what doesn't, students have offered insightful comments such as:

- "Feedback indicates the quality of my work."
- "Feedback helps me to elaborate on my ideas."
- "Feedback sounds like constructive criticism."
- "If I just get a grade and no comments, I don't know what to improve."
- "If I get my paper back after a week, it has no meaning since we are on to some other topic."

Feedback alone is powerful, and as previously mentioned, it can double the rate of learning for students (Wiliam, 2011). However, feedback must be given appropriately; more important, it must be *received* and *acted upon* by the receiver of the feedback. This applies equally to teachers and students. Turning a blind eye to the feedback and failing to act upon the information will yield no improvement. However, when teachers use feedback to change practices and even to seek and act upon negative feedback, the rate of student learning can increase substantially. In the research, this has been called "formative evaluation of teaching," and it has an effect size of 0.90, which equates to more than two years' growth in learning in one year's time (Hattie, 2012). To achieve this type of effect, teachers use feedback from student work, assessments, and comments from coaches or supervisors to change their instruction to better meet the needs of students. This reflective and formative element of feedback is what separates expert teachers from experienced teachers. It is not a secret to be held only by the elite and distinguished teachers. *Stepping into the minds of students and seeing through their eyes is something that can be learned, and is the catalyst to improving one's practice.*

## FEEDBACK DECONSTRUCTED

In order to make the most of feedback and formative evaluation of teaching in the classroom, we have synthesized the research and best practices into an easy to remember acronym, using the word *feedback* itself. Throughout the chapter, we will explore each descriptor to deepen our discussion of feedback and suggest ways to incorporate it into the classroom.

| F | E | E | D | B | A | C | K |
|---|---|---|---|---|---|---|---|
| Frequent | Efficacious | Exchange-Oriented | Differentiated | Balanced | Accurate | Criteria-Driven | Kinesthetic |

### FREQUENT: Recurrent, Common, Every Day

Because feedback for learning should answer the questions *Where am I going? How am I doing?* and *Where to next?*, the timing and frequency of feedback are critical to informing and empowering students to take the next steps in learning. One question that often comes to the forefront of the conversation is, "How often should feedback be offered and by whom?" Let's begin with the difference between immediate and delayed feedback.

A critical element to both immediate and delayed feedback being effective is the quality of the instruction being provided. If the instruction is meaningful and provides students with enough information to move forward in their learning, feedback then has the potential to be effective (Hattie & Timperley, 2007).

### *Immediate Feedback*

Assuming that the instruction is effective and meaningful, **immediate feedback** is often most helpful when students are first learning a new idea or performing a task for the first time. In this case, students need immediate feedback to affirm the new learning or provide them with accurate information about errors or misconceptions.

Consider a typical math lesson. The teacher has introduced the students to a new type of problem they must learn to solve. She has provided direct instruction and modeled her thinking to support students in preparing to solve problems on their own. Each student is given a whiteboard and asked to work a sample problem, and then check his or her answer with a partner. If the partner group finds their answers don't match, they can talk through how they each solved the problem, looking for errors and referring to the problems modeled by the teacher. If they are unsuccessful in determining the error, they can seek help from their teacher to determine where the misconception or error occurred, and then try another problem. This way, the feedback is immediate, and prepares the students to become more independent in solving the problems.

The teacher has also received immediate feedback (S: Embedded Formative Assessment) on the clarity of the instruction and modeling provided. By observing, listening to, and assisting the students, she can instantly decide the next steps when they struggle. If it is clear that a student has little or no understanding of what has been taught and seems totally lost, providing feedback is pointless. The student needs to be retaught, and most likely a different approach must be considered.

If the class as a whole demonstrate varying degrees of understanding and would benefit from additional modeling or practice, some possible actions might include:

- Have students identify what was most problematic in the problem-solving process and what they learned from their partner conversations.
- Ask specific students to model and explain their thinking as they move through the problem with you.
- Provide another problem or two for all to solve with a partner before moving on to independent work.
- Allow students to decide when to work independently, work with partners, or remain with you for more practice and feedback until they feel confident.
- Provide students illustrated answer keys so they can immediately check their work when they are practicing and learning new skills and concepts.

When all or the majority of students struggle, use a different strategy to reteach and model the process again with more scaffolding by stopping after each step and asking students to complete a portion of the problem before moving on to the next step. Allow students who appear to understand the process to elect to proceed on their own and to be able to immediately self-check their responses.

### Delayed Feedback

**Delayed feedback** tends to be more effective when students have a sound foundation in a concept or skill and are working to deepen their learning. Think back to Chapter 2, when the standards were placed along the continuum from surface to deep learning. As we transition from surface to deep learning, delayed feedback is often more effective.

Sometimes, we tend to focus on whether the answer is correct or not, and when it is, we push students on to the next standard or idea. Instead, consider supporting students in achieving deep understanding and letting them grapple with the learning in order to build skills as problem-solvers and understand the importance of persevering through challenges in learning. The writing process is a good example to consider how delayed feedback would be more effective than immediate feedback. It is difficult, if not impossible, to give corrective feedback before students have had time to plan their writing and begin an initial draft. If corrective feedback is immediate, a student's ideas may be cut short or be underdeveloped. In this case, it is more productive to give students time to process their thinking and planning with you or a peer. Engaging in a conversation with the writer regarding thought processes and ideas being developed will likely be more productive than providing feedback about specific writing criteria such as including a solid introduction, supporting details, and transition words.

### Structures for Feedback: Immediate and Delayed

We recommend that teachers establish consistent and useful structures for giving and receiving immediate or delayed feedback. These structures can become part of what is done every day or week to ensure that the lines of communication remain open and fluid as the student demonstrates progress toward achieving the Learning Intentions. Just as we teach students procedures for classroom routines such as entering and leaving the classroom, getting materials, turning in work, forming groups, and more, we also need to intentionally teach feedback structures and routines. Interestingly, this also relates to the S in the TRUST Model, which represents the structures component within the model. In Chapter 1, several ideas were shared about how to request and act upon feedback concerning the classroom culture. The following structures promote academic feedback.

### Time for Application

I. Questions for Discussion

Questioning is a very common practice teachers use to check understanding. If teachers are strategic, they and their students can receive valuable feedback on what is clear and unclear through the questions asked by students or the teacher and the responses. However, the quality of questioning is often lacking when trying to determine the level and depth of understanding students have reached. Shirley Clarke (2008) offers five models for developing effective questions to determine student understanding through discussion with peers:

- *A range of answers.* Ask a question and offer a range of possible answers from some that are correct, some that are not, and others that are partially correct. Students discuss the answers and come to a consensus on the accuracy of the answers, along with an explanation of why.
- *A statement.* Turn a question into an open-ended statement and ask students to build an argument around whether they agree or disagree.
- *Right or wrong.* Two opposites are presented to students, and they are asked to determine which is "right" and which is "wrong," and explain why.
- *Starting from the answer or end.* Answers are given to students in a way similar to the game *Jeopardy*, and students must provide the question.
- *An opposing standpoint.* Students are given two or more opposing viewpoints on a topic and asked to build a case from one viewpoint.

II. The Traffic Light

The traffic light is a structure that can be used daily at the end of class for feedback, and it has many variations. In one example, red represents things the student(s) didn't understand. Yellow represents learning that is still a bit fuzzy or somewhat unclear. Green represents what was understood and learned that day. The teacher asks students to respond orally or in writing to a series of prompts about the day's learning. For example, the teacher refers to a traffic light and asks students to respond to prompts for each color. The information gleaned from the writing samples or class discussion provides signals or feedback to the teacher to potentially adjust instruction for the next day. The following is a sample of the questioning prompts:

Green—What I learned or understand: _____

_____

Yellow—What I am unclear on or sort of understand: _____

_____

Red—What I don't understand: _____

_____

III. Personal Learning Target

In this structure, each student has a small target on his or her desk, and a game chip. For older students, the target could be posted in the room and provide a visual for a written or verbal "exit slip." Students are asked to place the game chip on the target to represent how well they understand the Learning Intention. If they don't understand, and need assistance or clarification right away, they move the chip toward the outside ring of the target. If they understand and are progressing well, they leave the chip at the center of the target. This signals to the teacher and peers when a student needs help and allows for targeted and immediate

**Figure 5.1**  Sample of Personal Learning Target

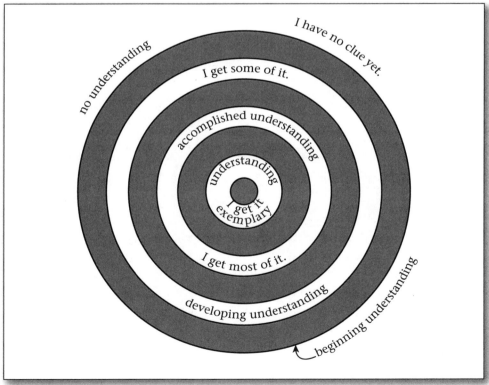

Used with permission of Amy Cosgrove.

feedback. (Structure designed by Amy Cosgrove, North Routt Community Charter, North Routt, Colorado.)

## EFFICACIOUS: Useful, Valuable, Successful

Students receive tons of feedback every day, as do teachers. The question is, *How useful is the feedback?* Nuthall found in observations of secondary classrooms that 80 percent of the feedback students receive every day is from their peers, and 80 percent of the time the feedback is wrong (2007). This is often due to the fact that the feedback is unclear, unkind, or lacks criteria to inform what was shared.

We also know that teacher feedback can be useless. How many times have we seen the following symbols or comments at the top of students' work? "Excellent," "Much better," "✓" "89%," "☺," "You need to try harder," or even "Baloney!" None of these comments do anything to further or nourish learning. In fact, some students may actually regress due to this type of feedback. Two important considerations that relate to the word *efficacious* are praise versus academic feedback and grades versus comments. Keep in mind that all of the other components in the acronym also relate to feedback being efficacious.

**Praise Versus Academic Feedback.** We all want to praise students and often find ourselves telling them they did a good job or were well behaved, but research has found some interesting correlations between praise feedback and feedback that is related to learning or academics (Hattie, 2012; Wiliam, 2011). You may also recall from Chapter 1 how something as seemingly innocuous as praise can contribute to a fixed mindset if combined with feedback on learning. The following criteria provide best practices around praise and academic feedback.

- Praise feedback, or feedback about the person, should be kept separate from academic or corrective feedback (i.e., "You are wonderful to have in class.").
- Praise feedback should praise effort so as to relate to something the students can control, rather than intelligence (i.e., "The long hours and effort you expended are directly related to your performance on this exam.").
- Academic feedback should meet the students where they are in their learning progression (i.e., "I see you have used some dialogue in your writing. Let's look at specific examples in our text to help you learn how to correctly format the dialogue.").
- When giving feedback, instead of providing students with the answer, scaffold the feedback so as to give them a step or a leg-up in

answering a problem or question on their own (i.e., "I see that you are trying to write your lab report. Please look at the Step 3 criteria and the example, and then revise this step to meet the expectations we discussed.").

**Grades Versus Comments**. We often combine comments and a grade when returning daily work and even assessments that are intended to be formative in nature. However, research has shown that if comments are given in order to further learning, marking the paper with a grade actually stops learning. It may seem surprising, but when a grade is included, students tend to ignore the written comments. If students receive a good grade, they often ignore the comments, feeling they have done well enough. On the other hand, if students receive a poor grade, they often feel dejected and won't even read the comments because they know they have already failed, and the comments only reinforce this feeling. *Therefore, grades should be given only on work that is truly summative, or at the end of learning, after there has been ample time to practice the learning and receive feedback.* Comments alone should be used on work that we hope students will use to further their learning (Wiliam, 2011).

What can replace grades during learning? The student goals template introduced in Chapter 3 is a good example of a tracking tool that can be used by teachers, students, and parents to determine progress toward the Learning Intentions. The students and teacher can use the tool to monitor the Learning Intentions and/or Success Criteria that have been reached and those that have not. In addition, student work samples with comments can be added, as suggested in Chapter 4, through the development of the learning portfolio. In this way, a great deal of information about learning can be shared—much more than is provided on a typical progress report. Instead of receiving a score of 54 percent, 85 percent, or 99 percent, which provides no information about what was and was not learned, a sampling of student work reveals what has been learned and what still needs to be learned for the teacher and the learner.

To bring this a little closer to home, imagine your students giving you a grade as a form of feedback about the quality of instruction they received today. It may seem ludicrous, but would receiving a C, F, or A provide any useful information to you about what was effective or ineffective in your lesson? Rather, consider how *efficacious* the feedback could be if students offered comments about what did or didn't work for them. They might comment on how your modeling and use of a think-aloud contributed to successful learning today during the group discussions. You now have useful feedback that informs you about your instructional practice and also about the effectiveness of group structures. More important, acting upon the students' feedback conveys the importance of the partnership and models how you value feedback from others.

## EXCHANGE-ORIENTED: Conversation, Interchange, Trading

Exchange captures the core of feedback by implying that there is a feedback loop or a two-way street in the teaching and learning process. In our work to identify Learner Strategies for students, feedback represents one of the most crucial strategies students can learn. Think of the life applications for learning how to effectively give and receive feedback. Students will be asked to use these skills in future schooling and careers, and in their home life as well. This idea transcends to many areas of their life, from thinking of themselves as learners in a new job to partners in a new marriage. Success in these arenas depends on an effective feedback exchange.

So much of the exchange hinges on how the feedback is given and received. Our goal is for feedback to be delivered appropriately, and acted upon so learning moves forward. However, the feedback exchange can actually impede learning if it is misunderstood, ignored, or simply rejected.

To illustrate how students can provide feedback to a teacher open to the exchange, consider Maria's story and think about how you might have responded. Maria, a kindergarten teacher, was in the middle of a lesson when a little boy suddenly raised his hand and said that he had no idea what she was talking about. She mentioned how it surprised her, but that she was glad he had stopped her to let her know. She then responded by asking the class if they felt the same way, and to explain what was confusing to them. She used their feedback to immediately adjust the manner in which she was teaching the Learning Intention. The information provided by this brave little kindergartner prompted Maria to reflect on future lessons she had planned and to make improvements. While this sounds wonderful, think of alternative ways she might have reacted. She could have asked the student to listen better and not interrupt, or made some other remark to save face. However, her response demonstrated that she too is a learner. She modeled for her students how to take honest feedback and use it to learn and improve.

Most students don't come preprogrammed with strategies for giving and receiving feedback; therefore, it is our job to teach them. We recommend both modeling and offering frames or structures for feedback. Let's look at an example, using a feedback technique called Two Wows and a Wish.

The structure calls for two positive comments to be given about a student's work or performance, and one constructive criticism to improve on the work or performance. One way to model this structure is for a teacher first to ask for feedback and then model using the structure. For example, the teacher first provides instruction about how to write an argument. He then asks the students for feedback on the instruction, using Two Wows and a Wish. He thanks the students for their honest feedback and explains how he will use the feedback to change his instruction next time. After modeling how to use the structure to give and receive feedback, he provides the students an opportunity to practice giving feedback to one another on their rough drafts, using Two Wows and a Wish. To help students structure the feedback, he asks them to review a limited number of paragraphs to offer one another feedback, based on the Success Criteria and in the structure of Two Wows and a Wish. Students are then given an opportunity to share their feedback and improve their writing, based on the affirmations and suggestions offered.

### *Time for Application*

I. Feedback Frames

You may be familiar with the use of sentence or summary frames to support language acquisition and struggling learners (Hill & Flynn, 2006). Why not teach your students feedback frames to give them the language needed to give and receive feedback? Without feedback frames, students may be overly blunt and say things like, "Wrong, wrong, wrong," or "I thought this idea was lame." Conversely, students may also not know how to provide constructive feedback and just offer a simple "I thought your work was really good." Neither scenario furthers learning. The following feedback frames provide sample sentence starters to offer students the language they need to give and receive feedback. After reading through the list of potential frames, you may want to add a few of your own and create a running list of tips or sentence frames with your students.

**Figure 5.2** Feedback Frames

| Giving | Receiving |
|---|---|
| I noticed that . . . | I appreciate you noticing that . . . |
| I wondered about . . . | I hadn't thought about that . . . |
| I was confused by . . . | I heard you say that _____ confused you. |
| I suggest that . . . | Based on your suggestion, I will . . . |
| Have you thought about . . . | If you were me, what would you do? |
| You might consider . . . | I'm not sure what that looks like. Tell me more. |

## DIFFERENTIATED: Discerning, Set Apart, Individualized

Many times, teachers will provide generalized feedback on homework, a quiz, or a test that sounds something like, *Most of the class did okay yesterday. There were a few areas in which many of you struggled. You need to reread and study the section on D-Day. I'll hand back your papers at the end of the class today for you to take home and study. As you know, about one-third of the content from this test will be on the final exam. However, the questions will be different.* How do you think students take this feedback? Is it meaningful to them? Do they feel it is just for them? The nature of this type of feedback is too global for students to derive any benefit from it. In fact, students tend to think the teacher is addressing someone else and will fail to sit up and take notice (Hattie & Timperley, 2007). Even if students have their papers right in front of them, the feedback will most likely fall upon deaf ears. Unless the work is accompanied with specific feedback, the papers with all the grading marks and comments will end up in the "round file," otherwise known as the trash bin. To be effective, feedback must be perceived as being personal and specific, and the timing must be appropriate for students to act upon the information. Students need to view feedback as "just for me," "just right," and "just in time." This type of feedback captures what is described as the Goldilocks principle, and is a simple way to remember the necessary components of differentiated feedback.

To have meaning and move learning forward, feedback must also be differentiated as students move through each of the cardinal points— North, East, South, and West—on the Learner's Internal Compass. Feedback provides students with the necessary prompts to be able to respond to the questions *What is my contribution? Where am I going? How am I doing?* and *Where to next?* Some of you might be freaking out, thinking, "How in the world am I going to differentiate my feedback for every single student I teach? It's hard enough to differentiate my lessons!"

Students who own their learning and are our partners share the responsibility for providing feedback to self and peers and acting upon the information. When learning is at the surface level, students can check most of their work with answer keys, Success Criteria, or even by comparing responses with peers. This is the easy part. The more difficult task is to empower students to recognize errors and how to rectify their misconceptions. For example, the desired student response would be: "I got a lot of the same type of problems wrong, or I seem to make the same type of errors. I'm either being careless, or I don't understand the concept and need to learn this again. I might first need to reread the text and examples and try the problems again. Maybe I'll ask a classmate to explain it to me or look at an online instructional video. If it still doesn't make sense, I'll ask the teacher for help." By providing students the opportunity to practice at the surface level, they learn the essential Learner Beliefs that empower them to self and peer assess, activate learning from mistakes, and deepen learning through authentic challenges.

*Error Detection Skills*

We can begin teaching students to flex their muscle by learning how to employ error detection skills. This can be accomplished in a variety of subjects. The basic components involve the teacher underlining or circling incorrect answers, punctuation, calculations, and so on. The students then receive their annotated papers and act as detectives to find, classify (Wiliam, 2011), and correct what was underlined or circled. As students become more skillful at detecting their errors, teachers will simply put a check (√) in the margin for errors, or write a note at the top of the paper stating, for example, "Please look at your responses to #3 and #5 and revise your work." Over time, as students improve their error detection skills, they can begin to provide this type of feedback for themselves or for their peers. Think about the papers you wrote in college. Even after using spell check, you may have made notes in the margins as you edited your own writing to signal a need to reword or revise your ideas.

Another variation comes from Dylan Wiliam's *Embedded Formative Assessment* (2011). He explains the method used by a Spanish teacher who underlined errors in students' writing. The students were then asked to classify what the errors were in terms of tense, gender, pronouns, and so on, and to fix the mistakes. By going back to *analyze* and *classify* the errors, the students were actively building their own knowledge of Spanish grammar rules that could be applied to future writing assignments. This is a powerful step that builds students' independence, and can be applied to any grade or content area.

*Interacting With Text: A "During Reading" Feedback Strategy*

When students read, they often encounter words and phrases that interfere with their ability to understand or make meaning. The graphic organizer in Figure 5.3 can be used with students to document key ideas and also issues they are encountering as they read complex text. It would be best

**Figure 5.3** Interacting With Text

| Interacting With Text | | |
|---|---|---|
| Vocabulary or language I didn't understand | | Ideas I didn't understand |
| Key ideas | Important details | Connections I made |
| Summary | | |

served in the later elementary grades and in middle and high school. As the students read and make notes on the organizer, the teacher may circulate around the room, glancing at the responses to assess and intervene as needed to offer feedback, ask questions, clarify ideas, and so on.

### *Time for Application*

I. Be a Detective

Error Detection methods provide a way to differentiate feedback while simultaneously developing students' metacognitive skills as they analyze, classify, and correct errors. Think about how you might begin introducing your students to one of the error detection methods discussed. Start slow and limit the number and type of errors you want students to address. Be sure to model the practice with your students and then provide ample time for students to practice and provide feedback to you on what they are learning as a result of the effort.

II. Annotating and Interacting With Text

Figure 5.3 provides one example of how students can interact with text to ensure they comprehend an author's meaning. There are numerous ways students might also annotate the text to provide differentiated feedback to the self and to the teacher. With colleagues, talk about the various methods each teacher uses to have students interact with text or annotate the text. Next, discuss how the *teacher* and *students* use this information as feedback to guide next steps in learning.

## BALANCED: Learner to Teacher, Teacher to Learner, Peer to Peer, Self

The idea of a teacher providing all the feedback students need is impossible. As previously mentioned, most of the feedback students receive is from other students; and, according to Nuthall (2007), most of this feedback is incorrect unless we intercede thoughtfully. A balanced approach to giving and receiving feedback is necessary. The success of the feedback exchange is dependent on the needs of the student and should ultimately be balanced and varied among peers, the self, and the teacher. As teachers, we recognize that we deepen our own understanding of concepts when we must explain or teach them to others. When students provide specific feedback to themselves or others, they must synthesize their understanding and offer an explanation that essentially teaches the concept. To balance feedback and expand the results, teachers can adapt techniques within their existing routines at the beginning, middle, and end of lessons to provide opportunities for students to seek feedback from the following:

- *Self:* Evaluating or using metacognitive strategies, seeking information or correctives, creating self-teaching or self-regulating situation.
- *Peers:* Clarifying information or processing aloud for confirmation, peer teaching.
- *Teacher:* Information gathering from interactions, questions designed to determine re-teaching needs, corrections to assignments, test and project evaluation (Pollock, 2012).

Take a moment for self-reflection. How many self- or metacognitive structures are embedded in what you and your students do on a regular basis? Which might be most useful to add? How do students engage in peer-to-peer feedback? Is it working in your classroom? How could it be improved? Finally, how are students receiving feedback from you, and what structures are you using to provide such feedback? After considering these questions, we suggest finding structures for balanced feedback in your areas of greatest need and then working to incorporate them into regular practice in your classroom.

### *Time for Application*

I. Feedback to Self: Worked Examples

Even very young students can learn to assess their own writing by using worked examples, also known as illustrated examples or exemplars. If students are given a set of examples that illustrate the progression from beginning stages of writing to proficient writing, they can learn to compare their work to the worked examples. Even kindergartners are able to determine where they are currently performing and describe what is different about the next level to guide their next steps (see Figure 5.7, a first-grade example under Criteria-Driven). If young students can master this skill, imagine what older students can do with exemplars plus Success Criteria that have been co-constructed! Providing illustrated examples also works effectively when we can offer students a visual representation of a learning progression, or multiple ways to approach a problem. For example, the use of multiple samples to show or contrast specific art forms, methods to solve math problems, science lab write-ups, and research projects can be quite effective.

II. Peer-to-Peer Feedback: Text Playback

This structure is done in pairs and involves retelling the main ideas and key details after reading a partner's writing. This allows the writer to hear what the reader gained from reading his or her work. It can uncover misconceptions, areas the reader found particularly interesting, areas that lacked detail, and more (Fisher & Frey, 2011). The same concept can be applied to a common text students have read and tailored to meet specific

Learning Intentions such as discussing the author's opinion and evidence or lack of evidence cited to support their claim.

III. Teacher Feedback: Sharing Thinking through Sticky Notes

A structure for teacher-to-student feedback involves having students generate their ideas on sticky notes while they read. Prior to independent reading, the teacher may define the types of ideas to include on the sticky notes. For example, if the class is working on character development, students may generate ideas about attributes of the characters, changes in characters, or ways some characters interact with others to reveal the plot. As the teacher circulates around the room, he or she can review the notes students are generating and offer feedback to deepen student thinking. To see this strategy in action, access the Edutopia video link to view "Making Sure They Are Learning" at www.corwin.com/partneringwithstudents.

## ACCURATE: Progress in Learning, Feedback Fit

The type of feedback each learner requires is dependent on where the student is within the learning progressions discussed in Chapter 2. This might appear to be a daunting task; however, it does not need to be complicated or overwhelming. Hattie and Timperley (2007) propose a simple but effective model for providing the right fit for feedback depending on the cognitive complexity or rigor of the task. When the learning is new or students are introduced to the content for the first time, they are considered to be at the *task,* or surface level. The feedback that is most helpful is direct, immediate, and corrective. It is important to provide feedback that tells the student he or she is doing the task correctly or incorrectly and to address any misconceptions very early in the learning process. It can be as simple as "yes, it is correct" or "no, it is incorrect." Whether the response was correct or incorrect, it is often helpful to ask students to explain how they know the response is correct or what they need to do to ensure a correct response. If the students are completely confused or unable to provide an adequate explanation as to how they arrived at a response, it may be best to reteach the concept.

As learners begin to gain confidence in how to accomplish a task, the next layer of feedback required is at the *process* level. Process feedback guides students to make connections, develop a deepened understanding of concepts, process ideas and the relationships to other ideas or concepts, and build strategies and routines.

As students progress to deep learning, they will reach the final feedback level, *self-regulation*. Students at this level are able to manipulate the task, apply a variety of self-directed strategies, make decisions, and regulate their learning. Self-regulated learners are able to focus on the task at hand and can monitor their own actions and behaviors; and, when confronted with additional information, they can consider what has worked in the past or design a completely new plan of action. In other words, self-regulated learners will push aside doubts and fears and take the first steps into unchartered new territory. They know they will learn from their mistakes along the way.

Consider once more the example of learning to drive a car. When learning to drive, most people don't just jump onto the highway and go for a road trip. Instead, learning to drive starts with simple things like how to turn the car on, put it in park, or pull onto the street. These components of how to drive are representative of the task level. In this case, the most useful feedback would be about how to operate the car and implement the rules of the road, not how to plan an extended road trip.

Once a person gets comfortable with the general operation of a vehicle and has learned the rules of the road, the type of feedback needed changes to match the level of learning, thus bringing us to the process level. Good questions for the driver at this point might be: "We will be exiting the highway to head to the mall. What do you need to anticipate now?" "What would you do if someone cut in front of you?" "How do you change your driving when on ice or snow?" or "How would you react if a stoplight fails to change because there is something wrong with it?" Each of these questions would cause the driver to think and deepen his skill as a driver.

Finally, when a driver reaches the self-regulation level, it might be time to suggest a road trip or a drive that would include some personal planning and decision-making. Feedback may change to questions like: "How far do you think it is possible to drive in one day without being too fatigued or falling asleep at the wheel?" "Which route do you plan to take, and why?" or "What alternative route might you suggest if there is construction or a road closure?"

You can see how it may be annoying to get task-level feedback when you are a self-regulated driver: "You are going to need to put your blinker on." "You need to merge now." Conversely, it would be completely unhelpful to receive feedback about the best ways to avoid a collision in the snow when a driver is not sure of how to drive a stick shift. How can we apply this model with our students?

Learning in the classroom is no different from this example. To know what type of feedback to provide, we must know where students are in their progress toward achieving the Learning Intentions. Feedback is an implicit part of continual, ongoing formative process that must be intentionally planned by the teacher. Accurate feedback requires teachers to see where students are in the learning progressions and meet their needs at that point in time.

Consider the following example. Then work to create your own to think through what types of feedback would be most useful to students.

**Figure 5.4** Science Example: Graphing Data to Support the Use of the Scientific Method

| Learning Progression | Feedback Level | Examples of Feedback |
|---|---|---|
| To make a graph that best represents the data | Task | • I see you have selected the appropriate type of graph for the data you collected. How did you know which to use?<br>• The data you plotted on the X and Y axes are incorrect. Tell me why you decided which axis to use for the data. |
| To use a graph to show your data that can inform further hypotheses to test based on the trends and patterns in the data | Process | • What patterns and trends does the graph show you? Continue this line of thinking to determine if there are other emerging trends in your data.<br>• How would you translate what you see in the graph to a new hypothesis? You seem to have thought through this carefully. |
| To develop a new hypothesis and collect, graph, and summarize your data to determine results and next steps | Self-regulation | • What does your most current data tell you about the accuracy of your hypothesis? It seems you have found some inaccuracies. Explain your thinking to me about how you might revise your hypothesis.<br>• What are your next steps in testing your hypothesis? It seems you have conferred with several peers to refine your next steps. Tell me more. |

*Surface to Deep Learning*

### *Time for Application*

I. Questions: Prompts for Providing Feedback

After thinking through each example, we suggest you try one of your own. Once you have determined the learning progression and Learning Intention you would like to address, develop questions for each feedback level that will prompt a student response for you to provide feedback at the task, process, or self-regulation level. If this is a new idea, consider trying your question prompts with only a few students to gauge their reactions to your questions and the feedback offered.

II. Feedback Tracker

Figure 5.5 provides a sample recording form to document the level of feedback being provided to students as they respond to the question prompts. To use the Feedback Tracker for multiple days, use a different-colored pen each day and note the date. This way, it is clear if and when the feedback to students moved from surface to deep. You will find a Feedback Tracker template at www.corwin.com/partneringwithstudents.

**Figure 5.5** Feedback Tracker: Tracking Feedback Levels

| Sample Prompts | Explain How Your Answer Is Correct or Incorrect | What Strategies Did You Use? | How Could You Apply This to Another Situation? |
|---|---|---|---|
| *Student names* | *Task level* | *Process level* | *Self-regulation* |
| Paul | ✓ (2/15)<br>✓ (2/17) | ✓ (2/20) | |
| Denae | ✓ (2/15) | ✓ (2/17) | ✓ (2/20) |
| Jaquan | | ✓ (2/15)<br>✓ (2/17) | ✓ (2/20) |

## CRITERIA-DRIVEN: Clarity, Alignment to Learning Intentions, Gauges/Drives Learning

Put simply, all the work around feedback is only useful if it moves learning forward, and in order to do so, feedback must answer the questions *What is my contribution? Where am I going? How am I doing?* and *Where to next?* Students receive a great amount of feedback every day, but often it fails to address their progress toward achieving the Learning Intentions. Our goal is to ensure that we spend the majority of our time giving feedback that addresses students' progress.

In answering the four questions on the Learner's Internal Compass, we must align the feedback to the level needed, based on where the student is performing and on the Success Criteria to ensure that quality academic feedback is given. Let's take a few minutes to explore how these are connected while reviewing a deeper explanation in Figure 5.6.

**Figure 5.6**   Criteria-Driven Feedback Aligned to Learner's Internal Compass

| Question | Answer | Explanation |
|---|---|---|
| *What is my contribution?* | The student response references Learner Beliefs and the Class Credo to monitor behavior and help others learn. | The student not only is self-regulated, but is also demonstrating many Learner Beliefs. |
| *Where am I going?* | The student response references Learning Intentions, Success Criteria, and personal learning goals for the unit of study. | If students are to understand where the learning is headed, they must know and be committed to the Learning Intentions for the class, as well as their personalized goals. |
| *How am I doing?* | Teacher or peer feedback is aligned to Success Criteria and at each student's level (task, process, and self-regulation). | Success Criteria are essential to clarify what is required to meet the Learning Intention(s). The level of feedback can then be matched to a student's performance level to best align to his or her needs. |
| *Where to next?* | Teacher or peer feedback aligned to Learning Intentions and Success Criteria yet to be achieved and at each student's level (task, process, and self-regulation). | The student is guided to think deeply about what is learned and to make connections and progress toward self-regulation to meet the Learning Intentions and Success Criteria. |

One pitfall that sometimes occurs is around the question *Where to next?* When teachers see that a student can solve a problem or complete a task, they may respond with more of the same: "Well done, you did 1–10. Now complete 11–30." When students hear this response, they believe that *Where to next?* simply means more work (Hattie & Timperley, 2007). Students therefore learn not to ask or seek next steps in their learning. They think, "Great, I finished the work and that is as far as I am going." We must be careful to ask ourselves, "Did my feedback deepen learning?" Instead, we want students to push toward deeper thinking when they ask *Where to next?* We must respond with opportunities to enhance, challenge, and move students toward greater autonomy if they are to learn to be self-directed and persist in learning. The practice of providing exemplars, models, or rubrics is designed to help students envision *Where to next?* in the process.

The following example is from Andrea Knight, a first-grade teacher and literacy coach working in Florida. She created the anchor papers depicted in Figure 5.7 to help engage her students in conversations about what constitutes good writing that meets or exceeds their grade-level expectations. In her blog she states, "I read each of the samples, and teams of students were challenged to study the stories, discuss their thinking, and put the stories in order from weakest to strongest." As the students

**Figure 5.7**  First-Grade Writing Anchor Papers

Photograph courtesy of Andrea Knight.

Photograph courtesy of Andrea Knight.

discussed the strengths of the three- and four-level papers (see Figure 5.7), Knight recorded their observations on sticky notes, or used arrows to highlight specific ideas to draw attention to Success Criteria that later became part of a rubric for students to assess their own writing. According to Knight, "It all started with an inquiry question: How do writers know if their stories are interesting and strong?" To learn more about how student learning increased, visit her blog, Creating Readers and Writers: Literacy for a Lifetime. You may access electronic links to Knight's posts on Pinterest and her blog at www.corwin.com/partneringwithstudents.

### *Time for Application*

I. Generating Success Criteria for Greater Learning

Take a moment to envision Knight's first-graders *competently* using the Success Criteria to assess their own writing, or working with a peer to provide feedback on their writing. What do you think you would see and hear from these first-graders? Generate a list all of the behaviors you would expect to see. You have just created a beginning list of what is needed for students to become criteria-driven and self-regulated. In other words, you have created the Success Criteria for students to be able to truly benefit from *criteria-driven feedback* and also be able to answer *What is my contribution? Where am I going? How am I doing? Where to next?* Now that you have gained greater clarity on the behaviors needed to provide effective feedback, you can engage your students in a similar activity that ultimately leads to improved work products and greater self-regulated learning.

## KINESTHETIC: Action-Oriented, Answers *Where to Next?*

- The bottom line with feedback is that it must cause action—thus the word *kinesthetic*. If we employ all the elements of powerful feedback discussed so far, we still must ask ourselves, *Is it working? Do I see my students making changes, deepening their learning, and asking more questions? Are the students reflecting on mistakes and engaging in further learning to ensure they can say "I've got it!"? Is the feedback impacting my instruction? How have I changed my instruction, incorporated students' ideas, and developed more robust structures to facilitate feedback?*
- If we think back to the TRUST Model, we can ask ourselves questions that will lead us to knowing our impact when it comes to feedback and the implementation of the collaborative culture that is relationship oriented emphasized in the TRUST Model. Review the following questions in Figure 5.8 to reflect upon the feedback practices that support the TRUST Model.

**Figure 5.8** Kinesthetic Feedback and the TRUST Model

| | Elements of the Trust Model | Reflection Questions About Feedback |
|---|---|---|
| **T** | **Talent**<br><br>Deliberate efforts to surface the talent each student brings to the classroom and continues to develop throughout the year | ☐ Is feedback working to build learner confidence and build a growth mindset?<br><br>☐ Are students more aware of their own Learner Beliefs and able to articulate what helped them learn?<br><br>☐ Are students tracking their success according to the goals they set? |
| **R** | **Rapport + Responsiveness**<br><br>Development of rapport and responsiveness with each student and among students | ☐ Are our relationships being strengthened through the use of feedback?<br><br>☐ Are we learning how to give and receive feedback in ways that encourage the feedback to be accepted and acted upon? |
| **U** | **"Us" Factor**<br><br>Developing a sense of team, community, and interdependency to achieve learning goals | ☐ Are we collaborating to support one another's learning?<br><br>☐ Are we all involved in giving and receiving feedback?<br><br>☐ Has our Class Credo evolved to reflect the changes in our beliefs and behaviors? |
| **S** | **Structures**<br><br>Implementation of specific procedures and structures to build relationships and manage learning | ☐ Have I established structures that are working to facilitate effective feedback to self, peers, and teacher?<br><br>☐ Have the structures we have established become part of our routine for providing feedback? |
| **T** | **Time**<br><br>Requiring patience, perseverance, and willingness to take risks | ☐ Is time being allocated to ensure that feedback is taking place, is effective, and causes deepened learning?<br><br>☐ Do we take time to reflect on what we have learned and how we have learned it? |

### *Time for Application*

I. FEEDBACK to Self

Have you ever heard the phrase, "If it isn't monitored, it won't happen"? We want to become masters of effective feedback in order to best support learning for our students and ourselves, and to do so, we must monitor our use of effective feedback practices. Use the FEEDBACK acronym under Summing Up: Learning Through Effective Feedback as Success Criteria to monitor your feedback practices. Think about a unit of study you recently taught. Look at each piece of Success Criteria to generate a concrete example that illustrates how you or your students demonstrated the criterion. Use the following questions to reflect on and consider potential changes in your practices:

- What do you notice about yourself and the students?
- Did you find an area where you excel and maybe one in which it was difficult to generate an example?
- What is the balance between the examples you generated for yourself and the examples from students? Is it balanced or out of balance?
- What will you continue doing, and what might you consider changing?

II. Feedback and the Learning Portfolio

An additional way to put feedback into action in a concrete and evidence-based way is to include it in the learning portfolio. The goal with the learning portfolio is to show learning, or to make it visible. Therefore, the portfolio should show evidence of mistakes and corrections, clarified misconceptions, rough drafts with feedback, pre-assessments, ongoing formative assessments with comments, metacognitive strategies and self-assessment, as well as any additional evidence of progress.

We encourage you to grow the portfolio from the elements already described in the previous chapter to include the feedback and examples of formative assessment shared by the teacher, student, and peers during the learning process. To this end, we hope you will ask students to include their "work in progress" that can later be paired with final drafts, post-assessments, final performances, and self-assessments to ensure that the progress made by students is clear to the students themselves, parents, and teachers. Therefore, the idea of adding feedback and formative assessment examples to the portfolio is to highlight the growth achieved from beginning to end, as illustrated in Figure 5.9 (see p. 123).

To further this idea, let's return to Jamie's example from Chapter 4. What artifacts might Jamie gather to provide evidence of her learning journey? In Figure 5.10 (see p. 124), a space is provided to identify artifacts you feel would be most important for Jamie to consider collecting that would provide evidence of her learning journey. Once you have reviewed the sample, draft a list of artifacts specific to your classroom and unit of study that students may work to collect throughout the learning process in order to show progress.

**Figure 5.9**  Artifacts for the Learning Portfolio

| 1 | 2 | 3 | 4 | 5 |
|---|---|---|---|---|
| Student goals template *(including the Learning Intentions, Success Criteria, and personalized learning goals)* | Learning maps, work samples, homework, practice, photos, rough drafts, pre-assessment, etc. | Strategies for learning that also include Learner Beliefs | **Evidence of feedback, aligned to Success Criteria** | |

## SUMMING UP: LEARNING THROUGH EFFECTIVE FEEDBACK

Making the most of feedback is no easy task, and we realize that many factors play a role in the effectiveness of feedback. Learning how to give and receive feedback is an essential Learner Strategy. It is a skill that will serve students well into their adult lives. We recommend keeping it simple by recalling the Goldilocks principle: In order for feedback to be effective and *acted upon*, it must be viewed as *just right, just in time, and just for me*. Effective feedback can nourish unprecedented growth in learning for all students and teachers. Start with a few areas or with a few ideas offered in this chapter and build from there. Find what works and reimagine what doesn't. When all else fails, ask the students what they think. They are our best assets in the classroom and can partner with us to make feedback great.

As we come to the close of this chapter, we revisit the acronym FEEDBACK. The definitions provide the criteria for success to guide your thinking and planning as you work to implement powerful feedback practices. Use the Next Steps template to record your next steps.

### Success Criteria for Effective Feedback Practices

❑ FREQUENT—Feedback in my classroom is intentional and responsive to students' need for immediate and delayed feedback.

❑ EFFICACIOUS—Feedback is focused on academic progress, not the person, and is given without grades to encourage students to review, reflect upon, and act upon the feedback.

❑ **EXCHANGE-ORIENTED**—The exchange of feedback has been modeled, and students have been provided with structures that allow them to be part of the exchange.

❑ **DIFFERENTIATED**—Feedback is personalized and aligned to the needs of each learner, and students have been given effective strategies to offer immediate feedback to self and peers.

❑ **BALANCED**—Feedback is balanced between self, peer, and teacher.

❑ **ACCURATE**—Feedback is targeted at a level most appropriate for each learner and works to deepen learning.

❑ **CRITERIA-DRIVEN**—Feedback is based on the Success Criteria to ensure a clear understanding of what is expected for proficiency.

❑ **KINESTHETIC**—The elements of the TRUST Model establish the right environment for feedback to be received and acted upon.

## Next Steps: A Template for Reflection and Planning

*How can feedback propel learning forward for teachers and students?*

| Teacher's Role | Student's Role |
|---|---|
| Learning on the Journey: | Learning on the Journey: |

**Figure 5.10** Applying Learner Strategies and Collecting Artifacts

| **Name:** Jamie, Grade six | **Class/Period:** English Language Arts, Fourth Period |
|---|---|
| **Learning Intentions Demonstrated on the Pretest** <br><br> • To explain how the plot moves a story along <br> • To describe how characters are affected by the events in the story <br> • To show how different parts of a story affect its meaning and the way the whole story turns out | **My Personal Learning Goals** <br><br> • I need to work on reading the text to better understand how the main character is affected by the events and how to explain that using examples from the story. <br> • I need to work on how different phrases and words the author uses have an effect on the plot. I get how events affect the plot but never really thought about how the words the author uses make a difference. |
| **Success Criteria** <br><br> • Describe how the time and place a story takes place can affect the type of conflict or problem the main character(s) face. <br> • Connect the problem in the story to the events that led up to the climax. <br> • Show how the resolution ties up the story and resolves the problem or conflict for the main character(s). <br> • Connect the problem/conflict in the story to the resolution to show how the main character(s) changes. <br> • Show how other characters in the story interact during the events of the story and how their actions can affect the main character(s). <br> • Explain how the author uses word choice to shape the message in the story. <br> • Explain how each chapter relates to the others in order to move the plot along. <br> • Describe how the story would be different if particular scenes were missing from the text. | **Beliefs That Will Support My Learning** <br><br> • I will ask for suggestions and feedback to be sure I am reaching my learning goals. <br> • I will listen to others because I know we can learn from one another. <br> • I know that learning is hard work, and that when I struggle through problems I am becoming a better learner. <br><br> **Learner Strategies (see the list you generated in Chapter 4)** |
| **Potential Artifacts From the Learning Journey** <br><br> (Work samples, homework, practice, photos, rough drafts, pre-assessment, written reflections, etc.) | |

# Part III

# Retracing and Extending the Journey

# 6 Retracing Evidence to Prove and Extend Learning

*How can students and teachers prove deep learning has occurred?*
*How can proving Learner Strategies lead to deepened ownership of learning?*

> *Not everything that can be counted counts and not everything that counts can be counted.*
>
> —Albert Einstein

So often in schooling, once the post-assessment is given, we are off and running to the next unit of study, leaving little time for reflection of learning, asking deeper questions, clarifying long-standing misconceptions, or solidifying what worked and didn't work during the learning process. Therefore, as the class moves on to new standards and ideas, questions linger. For students, those questions may be whether they actually achieved the Learning Intentions, or wondering about something that they never fully understood. Students may think, "I got an 80% on the test, but I'm not sure what that means I learned." On the flip side, teachers may question if the strategies and experiences they planned really moved learning forward or not. We often leave the unit of study wondering if learning is proven, reflected upon, or

"Encouragement of learning utilizes content not as an end but as a means, where deep learning and 'learning to learn' ideally replaces surface learning and 'being taught.'"(Cornelius-White & Harbaugh, 2010, p. 102)

translated into strategies that can be employed for the future. At the heart of this internal debate are two critical questions both the teacher and the student can address on the Learner's Internal Compass: *How am I doing?* and *Where to next?*

We suggest diving deeper into our learning as teachers and students by establishing time for two meaningful steps:

- Students and teachers take time to prove learning by aligning evidence of learning to the Learning Intentions.
- Students and teachers also take time to solidify their understanding of the strategies that were critical in achieving the Learning Intentions and that could be used for future learning.

Taking the time to prove learning also aligns to the TRUST Model to continually build and grow relationships through a partnership of learning. In Figure 6.1, take a few moments to review how the TRUST Model can be used to prove learning.

**Figure 6.1** TRUST Model and Proving Learning

| | Component | Explanation That Aligns to Proving Learning | Explanation That Aligns to Proving Learner Strategies |
|---|---|---|---|
| **T** | **Talent**<br><br>Deliberate actions to discover and develop the *Talent for learning* in every learner. | Students and teachers reflect on learning to determine how students' Talent for learning and Learner Beliefs enabled them to reach the Learning Intentions. Confidence grows as students realize their accomplishments. | As students gain Learner Strategies their confidence is also boosted, and they are more prepared to tackle future challenges. |
| **R** | **Rapport + Responsiveness**<br><br>The ability to build relationships of trust and mutual respect and to respond or react appropriately to support learners. | By taking the time to prove learning, teachers communicate to students that they respect and honor their efforts to accomplish the Learning Intentions. A plan to address Learning Intentions not achieved at this time can also be | Building students' toolboxes for future learning communicates that a teacher not only cares about today's learning, but that all students develop skills and strategies to become lifelong learners. |

| | Component | Explanation That Aligns to Proving Learning | Explanation That Aligns to Proving Learner Strategies |
|---|---|---|---|
| | | discussed. Students' commitment to learning grows due to the teacher's responsiveness. | |
| U | **"Us" Factor** <br><br> A shared belief that everyone can learn and everyone is a vital contributor to the learning process. | Through classroom discussions, students describe how they supported and learned from one another throughout the learning process. Students share how they addressed mistakes and misconceptions, collaborated, and worked hard to learn more effectively. By taking time to prove learning as a group and participate in shared reflection, each learner realizes his or her contribution to the learning. | Students recognize that collaboration is a powerful, lifelong Learner Strategy. Through collaboration and teamwork, students learn new ideas, methods for learning, problem-solving approaches, and the importance of effective communication. The "Us" Factor provides richness in learning that could not be achieved in isolation. |
| S | **Structures** <br><br> The methods, procedures, and practices that enable students to be partners in the learning process and to own their learning. | By reflecting on the structures that supported learning, students and teachers develop a deeper understanding of what worked to move learning forward and what could be improved in the future. | Students learn collaborative skills essential to teamwork and partnering. They learn to manage conflict, new ways of thinking, and strategies to solve problems. |
| T | **Time** <br><br> The requirement of purposeful and intentional time dedicated to building collaborative relationships and developing Learner Beliefs and actions. | Dedicating time for students to reflect individually and collectively provides opportunities to celebrate the journey, changes in Learner Beliefs, and the contributions of others. It can also inform both the teacher and the student of problematic areas that need to be addressed in the future. | Teachers and students need time to intentionally make connections and think about one's own learning. This provides a chance to reflect, to learn, and to make choices or changes regarding personal learning goals or behaviors. Deliberately engaging in metacognition is a strategy that can save instructional and learning time in the future if done deeply and regularly. |

## PROVING LEARNING THROUGH A BODY OF EVIDENCE

The first formal step in proving learning is to select and organize evidence that has been gathered throughout the unit of study. Students will align the evidence with the Learning Intentions to prove what was learned and what remains to be learned. What evidence can be included? The post-assessment, once administered, scored, and returned to students, can provide *one* form of evidence of learning. The post-assessment may be a performance assessment or a written assessment, but either way, it should reflect the Learning Intentions or expected outcomes. However, the *post-assessment alone is not proof of learning*; rather, it is a snapshot of learning. To build a **body of evidence**, other forms of student work are required and may include daily work, homework, performance tasks, written reflections, and more; therefore, it provides the photo album that includes multiple forms of evidence that proves student learning. The process of selecting the right evidence to include spurs reflection on what was learned and the strategies that promoted learning. The evidence should go beyond the "pretty pieces" of student work and must also include many of the items considered "work in progress," such as a first draft that includes comments and corrections paired with the final draft. Just as explorers kept journals, logs, and artifacts from their travels, we are documenting the journey of learning by looking for progress to be proven, not just the end result.

We recommend that teachers begin by providing students with an organizational structure and time to organize the learning portfolios at the beginning of every new unit of study. As students become more familiar with the process, they may offer alternate organizing structures to meet their needs or the requirements of a specific unit of study. For example, a writing portfolio and a science portfolio may require different organizational formats. Students and teachers can work together to collect and organize the evidence. In Figure 6.2, we now have all the components necessary to guide the development of learning portfolios that may take many shapes and forms.

As the evidence is gathered, students may be asked to review the Student Goals Template and

"What is often left out of the formula in student portfolios—though the trend is rapidly changing—is an intentional primary focus not on skills development, but on the learning process. The learning focus entails the deliberate and systematic attention to a student's self-reflective, meta-cognitive appraisal of what was learned, how it was learned, when it was learned best, and more importantly, why this learning is valuable. Such meta-cognition—that is, thinking about thinking, learning about learning, focusing on the process of learning as an enriching complement to content knowledge and skills as products of education—is central to how and why portfolios deepen learning." (Zubizarreta, 2008, p. 2)

**Figure 6.2** Artifacts for the Learning Portfolio

| 1 | 2 | 3 | 4 | 5 |
|---|---|---|---|---|
| Student Goals Template (*including the Learning Intentions, Success Criteria, and personalized learning goals*) | Learning Maps, work samples, homework, practice, photos, rough drafts, pre-assessment, etc. | Strategies for learning that also include Learner Beliefs | Evidence of feedback aligned to Success Criteria | **Final products, performances, and/or post-assessment** |

Learning Map to reflect on the Learning Intentions established during the unit or for various chunks of learning. Ask students to provide evidence from their work to prove they met and achieved each Learning Intention. In this process, students reflect on their work, make connections, and determine what they have accomplished.

Is it a good use of time in our classrooms to have students create learning portfolios? If you want deep and long-lasting learning, the answer is yes. How often have students said, "Why are we doing this assignment?" "I never got that paper back, so I am not sure how I did." "I don't know if I met the Learning Intentions because I got a 70% on the post-assessment; I guess I learned some of them." "My final project shows I know this stuff, but I didn't do that well on the test!" From each of these comments, it is evident that there is a disconnect. We want students to be able to answer *Where am I going? How am I doing?* and *Where to next?* Without providing the time for reflection of learning, how will students know if learning has moved forward, and which strategies worked or didn't work? It is reminiscent of when an author fails to wrap up a book and leaves the reader hanging and perplexed. The same applies for students. We can no longer leave them hanging, wondering if they actually accomplished the Learning Intentions, let alone exceeded them.

This is especially true when students set their own goals and personalize the Learning Intentions. Honoring their commitment to their goals will provide feedback on the importance of persistence, grit, and following through to meet the goal. It will communicate that we care, and that we deeply want to see each student be successful. If students never answer the question of whether goals were achieved, we will see students decline future challenges or refuse to set lofty goals because we didn't honor their commitment. We will also see that students stop progressing toward becoming self-regulated learners.

Once the learning portfolios have been organized, and include the required evidence to prove learning, students and teachers are poised to engage in a variety of actions to verify learning, reflect on the process, and determine next steps. These may include self, peer, teacher-and-student, whole-class, and external reflections, which may involve sharing work with another class, the school, and parents through student-led conferences. By engaging in such activities, students and teachers are learning to think about their own thinking, or **metacognition**. The process of engaging in metacognitive reflection while proving one's own learning solidifies *what was learned* and *how it was learned*. "Making students' thinking visible serves a broader educational goal as well. When we demystify the thinking and learning process, we provide models for students of what it means to engage with ideas, to think, and to learn" (Ritchhart, Church, & Morrison, 2011, p. 28).

Figure 6.3 includes a practical application for each type of reflection to start the process. There are numerous ways to engage in the process of proving learning, and we invite you to generate additional ideas. These questions can also be applied as a midpoint review of the learning

**Figure 6.3**  Types of Reflection to Prove Learning

| Types of Reflection | Practical Application |
| --- | --- |
| Self | Students review the evidence of their work collected over time and check off each Learning Intention or personal goal that has been met as evidence to prove learning. Students then determine *Where to next?* for their learning. |
| | *Self-Reflection Questions:* Which Learning Intentions have I accomplished and have evidence to prove my learning? What do I still need to learn to achieve the Learning Intentions? Who can help me, or do I just need more practice? When do I think I can fully achieve the Learning Intentions and my personal goals? Which Learner Beliefs and Learner Strategies did I demonstrate? How can I share my learning? |
| Peer | Students review the learning portfolio with a peer and offer feedback as to whether the evidence clearly shows the Learning Intentions or personal goals have been met. Students consider how they are contributing to one another's learning and Learner Beliefs. The students consider and discuss the effect of the Learner Strategies being used. |
| Teacher and student | The teacher confers with students to review evidence and discusses which Learning Intentions have been accomplished and what still needs to be achieved. Students also provide feedback about their instructional needs in order to reach the Learning Intentions. Both the teacher and the students are learning how they can improve learning to determine *Where to next?* Students and teachers reflect on the Learner Beliefs that have surfaced as Talent for learning. |

| Types of Reflection | Practical Application |
|---|---|
| Whole class | The teacher engages the students in a conversation to solicit the Learner Beliefs and Learner Strategies that are being activated as they assemble their portfolios to prove learning. Teachers can also create a *data wall* to display students' progress toward meeting personal goals, the Learning Intentions, or specific Success Criteria. It is important to note that the data posted do not include specific test results or any data that would violate a student's right to privacy or potentially cause embarrassment. For example, the information posted on a data wall might show the percentage of students who have documented a particular Learner Belief, or perhaps the number of students who have accomplished 80, 90, or 100 percent of their personalized learning goals over the course of a unit of study. By graphing this data for all to see and *also* posting anecdotal comments from students about strategies being used, it can demystify *how* students are able to make significant learning gains. This can be an insightful and powerful motivator for students. |
| External | Students may lead conferences with their parents or other significant adults to prove their learning and show how they achieved the Learning Intentions by meeting the Success Criteria. These conferences can be conducted at school, replacing or supplementing the traditional parent–teacher conference. However, student-led conferences could be conducted more frequently and independently among students and parents or other significant adults during and after each unit of study. Not only would students have an opportunity to hone their presentation skills, the adults would have more information about what students are learning and how they are learning. As students are able to articulate their own learning, they are able to show what they know and how they have learned. |

portfolio—or, even more frequently, to help students refine the process and reflect on their learning and the evidence.

After proving one's learning, it may be evident that some misconceptions or a lack of understanding have kept a student from fully reaching his or her goals. This presents an incredibly important opportunity for the teacher and students to make a plan to close the gap. Because both teacher and student are well informed about how closely the student has or has not come to reaching the Learning Intentions and meeting personal learning goals, a powerful conversation can then take place about *Where to next?* Ainsworth (2010, 2015) suggests that at the end of each unit of study, a buffer or bridge time is scheduled to allow for reteaching students who have yet to accomplish the Learning Intentions, and also provide enrichment or extended learning for students who are ready. This scheduled time affords teachers the chance to respond to the well-defined needs of students and supports the response to intervention process established at most schools.

*Time for Application*

I. A Living TRUST Model

Think about a unit of study you will teach and how to use the TRUST Model to apply the knowledge you are developing. As you plan how students will progress through the unit, consider how students can prove learning and also surface the strategies used to achieve the Learning Intentions. Refer to Figure 6.1, TRUST Model and Proving Learning, to create a blank template. Begin drafting your ideas about how students will demonstrate each element of the TRUST Model as they *prove their learning* and *the strategies* used to achieve the Learning Intentions of the unit.

II. Building Learning Portfolios for Your Classroom)

All the components of a Learning Portfolio have been discussed and illustrated to provide a basic structure for your consideration. Take time to contemplate how you will implement learning portfolios as you think about the age of your students, resources available, and familiarity with technology. Think carefully about how you will introduce the portfolio and involve students in determining the design and contents of the learning portfolio. Feel free to make changes or adapt the portfolio as you and the students learn from this experience.

III. Reflection of Learning

When asking students to reflect on how they are proving their learning, there are four different audiences to consider, as illustrated in Figure 6.3. As you think about a unit of study you will teach, generate multiple ways students can reflect on how they can prove their learning. Think carefully about what you will need to have in place for students to engage in a conversation with the self, peer, teacher, class, or other significant adults.

# PROVING LEARNING TO EMPOWER FUTURE LEARNING

Proving learning also allows students and teachers time to build a Learner Strategies toolbox. When the Learning Intention is aligned to student work that proves learning, students and teachers can then make powerful connections about what worked to move learning forward.

For the teacher, engaging in reflection with students regarding the effectiveness of the instructional structures and strategies used throughout the unit provides meaningful evidence of what worked best, as well as potential changes for future instruction. If teachers skip this step, they are left to infer what was or was not effective based upon observations and assessment results alone. However, by asking students to offer feedback and linking their comments to instructional practices, teachers gain a deeper under-standing of which learning structures and strategies worked best and what changes are necessary. As a result, teachers receive a more complete picture that informs future decision-making about instructional practices.

For the students, providing feedback to the teacher while proving learn-ing solidifies their important role in the classroom as partners in learning who also contribute to their teacher's success. In addition, it teaches them to be reflective and thoughtful learners, and ultimately leads to development of Learner Strategies. As students reflect on and think about what worked and what didn't work to move learning forward, the learner toolbox grows. For example, some students might discover they learn much better when they are able to draw concepts being taught or create a comparison matrix rather than use Venn diagrams. Once realized, students are then able to determine how to select and apply the most useful strategies from their own toolbox for use in future learning situations. As a consequence, they are developing metacognitive skills that lead to becoming self-regulated learners.

It is also important for students and teachers to consciously note the Learner Beliefs that are being developed as *Talent* for learning described in the TRUST Model in Chapter 1. In Figure 6.4 (see p. 136), take a moment to make an explicit connection between a Learner Strategy and the Learner Belief statement. Students need these same opportunities to make con-scious connections between beliefs that support learning and the strategies that activate learning. Often, teachers will post the Learner Belief such as, "I assess my own work to determine what I know and need to know." Capturing these statements and examples from students throughout the teaching and learning cycle reinforces the metacognitive connections. Just as students need multiple opportunities to practice and refine any new skill, they will also need multiple opportunities to express the Learner Beliefs and strategies in a variety of ways.

We can support students in adopting strategies into their learner toolbox in two ways: (1) proving learning through aligning evidence and Learner Strategies to the Learning Intentions, and (2) determining which Learner Beliefs were critical to getting the most out of each strategy. Take a few moments to review the examples of Learner Strategies and the Learner Beliefs to determine how a reflection of both could empower students for future learning.

How do we get started with this portion of proving learning? Essentially, we ask students to take the reflection process one step further by asking, "What strategies used in our classroom empowered you to meet each of the Learning Intentions?" Students are then asked to link the strategies to the evidence of learning in order to realize effective strategies that should be incorporated into their personal learning toolbox. In Figure 6.5, we have

**Figure 6.4**  Learner Strategies and Learner Beliefs

| Examples of Learners Strategies | Learner Beliefs |
|---|---|
| <ul><li>Setting personal learning goals</li><li>Assessing prior knowledge</li><li>Planning strategies to tackle a task</li><li>Organizing information (using a Learning Map)</li><li>Problem-solving</li><li>Note-taking</li><li>Self-teaching</li><li>Modeling</li><li>Non-linguistic Representations</li><li>Reciprocal teaching</li><li>Summarizing learning</li><li>Metacognition/Reflection of learning</li><li>Discussion strategies</li><li>Collaboration skills</li><li>Research strategies</li><li>Help-seeking</li><li>Leadership skills</li><li>Self-assessment of learning and strategies</li></ul> | <ul><li>I seek evidence to determine if I am reaching my learning goals.</li><li>I know that if I didn't learn it today, I can try a new method tomorrow.</li><li>When I am in the classroom my conversations are focused on learning.</li><li>I see the work and tests in my class as information to me about what I have and have not yet learned.</li><li>I listen to others because I know we can learn from one another.</li><li>I enjoy challenge and persist to find solutions to the problems.</li><li>I trust myself, my peers, and my teacher as teammates in learning.</li><li>I am comfortable taking risks and know that when I make mistakes, it helps me learn.</li><li>I know that learning is hard work and that when I struggle through problems, I am becoming a more skillful learner.</li></ul> |

**Figure 6.5**  Learner Reflection and Applications

| Types of Learner Reflection | Practical Application |
|---|---|
| Linking strategies to learning | *Literal or Virtual Toolbox of Strategies:* Young students can be given the materials to make a toolbox to house strategies that have worked for them. These students might draw pictures of a Learner Strategy to put in their toolbox. Students might even use a recipe box with index cards to describe all the ways to seek help, to be filed under "need help." Older students might use an Excel spreadsheet to list strategies they find useful. Categories can be easily added, changed, and sorted to find Learner Strategies under headings such as "note-taking," "comparison organizers," "synthesizing information," or "study ideas." They may also collect samples of how a strategy is to be used, such as in Figure 4.7, which explains how Learning Maps may be used. At the end of each unit of study, time can be spent adding or organizing Learner Strategies. |

| Types of Learner Reflection | Practical Application |
|---|---|
| Linking Strategies to Learning (cont.) | *Classroom Strategies Wall:* Together, the class can design a strategies wall that provides a resource for students to access different types of strategies they may choose to use for learning. Types of strategies may be organized by topics such as "organizational strategies," "feedback starters," "mnemonics," "summary writing," "problem-solving," or "research steps," and then reorganized as the need surfaces.<br><br>*Strategies Section in the Learning Portfolio:* As previously mentioned, students can also use the learning portfolio as a place to house the strategies that work best for their learning. This offers an easy place for students, teachers, and parents to access, add to, connect to evidence, and revise strategies. |

| Teacher Reflection | Practical Application |
|---|---|
| Log of powerful strategies | As teachers learn from students the practices that worked and didn't work, they become privy to insights that can revolutionize their teaching. During the reflection process of effective Learner Strategies, teachers should log what worked, why, and for what purpose to build their own toolbox of strategies that empower student learning. The following provides an example of how a teacher might create a log in a lesson plan book or journal. A similar organizational format could also be used for a strategies wall in the classroom. |

| Strategy | Why It Works | Purpose |
|---|---|---|
| Co-constructing Success Criteria | Students shared that it helped them understand what they needed to do to be successful. | Use at the beginning and during any unit to define learning. |
| Nonlinguistic representations (*pictures, diagrams, drawings, etc.*) | Students reported that it helped them make a mental picture of a word or concept. | Use with vocabulary, capturing an event or a major concept. |
| Memory aids (songs, acronyms, jingles, etc.) | Students stated that creating a rap or jingle helped them remember the content. | Use to help remember multiple steps, key words/phrases for concepts, or facts. |

provided several examples that describe how students and teachers can surface strategies that impact learning.

### Time for Application

I. Connecting Learning to Strategies: Students

Hopefully you have been inspired to think about ways to help students share and catalog their Learner Strategies. Perhaps you will work with a colleague to plan how to will involve students in creating a personal toolbox, a strategies wall, or how strategies will be noted in a learning portfolio. Be creative and be sure to invite the students to be part of the design and development phase to build ownership as they connect the dots between Learner Strategies and Learning Intentions.

II. Connecting Learning to Strategies: Teachers

Just as students are connecting the dots between strategies employed and the effect on learning, you will also be making connections between *how* you taught and the subsequent *impact* your students' learning. If you are thoughtful in your approach and open to feedback from your students, you will experience unprecedented growth as a teacher that will spur even greater growth in your students. The first step is to consciously build your toolbox. Make a commitment to create a learning log for yourself as suggested in Figure 6.5 and as you record and reflect on your strategies, make a conscious transition to the Learner's Internal Compass and ask yourself: *Where am I going? How am I doing? Where to next? What is my contribution? Am I empowering students to achieve worthy goals?*

## THE IMPACT ON STUDENTS

In the end, after expending all the time and energy to ask students to prove their own learning, *Does it matter? Does it have an impact on students and learning*? The answer is a resounding *yes*! The Quaglia Institute on Student Aspirations in its annual report on student voice (2013–2014) has identified eight conditions for success in terms of students realizing and accomplishing their aspirations. Most notably, the eight include a sense of accomplishment, leadership and responsibility, and confidence to take action, all of which define why proving one's learning is so empowering. We are building our students' confidence in their ability to reach worthy goals that cannot be faked, taken away, or changed by anyone. In this book, we have defined the Learner's True North as empowering students to own learning to achieve worthy goals with confidence and wisdom. In the achievement of these goals, students can build their life's aspirations on the back of their hard work and effort, proving they can learn and take responsibility to own and accomplish ambitious goals in preparation for future challenges.

Interestingly, the Quaglia Institute has found a strong correlation between having life aspirations and being engaged and motivated in school. In fact, students who have aspirations are eleven times more likely to be academically motivated than are students who don't have aspirations. However, aspirations do not offer a full picture of student motivation. Students who feel they have a voice in school are seven times more likely to be academically motivated. As teachers, we have an awesome and weighty opportunity to change futures by encouraging students to dream, plan, partner, own, and realize their future aspirations to equip them as skilled learners along the way:

> Instead of covering the curriculum and judging our success by how much content we get through, we must learn to identify the key ideas and concepts with which we want our students to engage, struggle, question, explore, and ultimately build understanding. Our goal must be to make the big ideas of the curriculum accessible and engaging while honoring their complexity, beauty, and power in the process. Where there is something important and worthwhile to think about and a reason to think deeply, our students experience the kind of learning that has a lasting impact and powerful influence not only in the short term but also in the long haul. They not only learn; they learn how to learn. (Ritchhart, Church, & Morrison, 2011, p. 26)

## SUMMING UP: RETRACING EVIDENCE TO PROVE AND EXTEND LEARNING

As a reflection of the journey, consider how proving one's learning brings learners full circle to realize what they have achieved and how they have accomplished the learning. Each of the compass points for the teacher and learner has been in play. Take a moment to think through the Learner Beliefs, TRUST Model, and compass points to determine if we have fully realized our goal to empower students to be our partners in learning.

**Teacher's Internal Compass**          **Learner's Internal Compass**

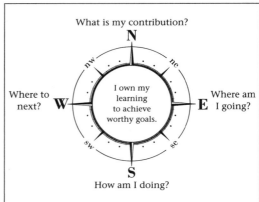

Use the following template to reflect on and plan how you will implement one to three actions, and what you expect from your students as you begin retracing evidence to prove and extend learning.

### Next Steps: A Template for Reflection and Planning

*How can students and teachers prove deep learning has occurred?*

*How can proving Learner Strategies lead to deepened ownership of learning?*

| Teacher's Role | Student's Role |
|---|---|
| Retracing and Extending the Journey: | Retracing and Extending the Journey: |

# 7 Retracing and Extending the Process

## A Summary to Guide Teachers and Leaders

*How can I leverage the strengths of all to take action?*
*How can the compasses guide collective action?*

—————— ✤  ✤  ✤  ✤ ——————

*When you improve a little each day, eventually big things occur. Not tomorrow, not the next day, but eventually a big gain is made. Don't look for the big, quick improvement. Seek the small improvement one day at a time. That's the only way it happens—and when it happens, it lasts.*

—John Wooden, head basketball coach, UCLA

In coming to the end of this book, we arrive at a place that requires reflection and action. As you contemplate your next steps, we hope you remember John Wooden's advice (Gallimore & Tharp, 2004). We must recognize that improvement is a continuous process that takes time and requires incremental steps every day. It begins with a commitment to take action and stay the course no matter how difficult, discouraging, or challenging the journey becomes on any given day. Although you will be thinking about your own classroom and a group of students, perhaps there are some nagging thoughts: *What happens after my students leave me? Will they rise up and demand to be included as partners in every classroom, or will they simply accept the status quo and fade back to being as they were before? Should this be a bigger, more systemic effort for my team, our school, or our district?* These are all important questions to address as we think about extending the journey. For now, we will focus on synthesizing *your* learning. Later in the chapter, we will address how partnering with students to build ownership of learning can have a greater and longer-lasting impact on students once they leave your classroom.

Hopefully, you have sampled some of the exercises, titled *Time for Application*, throughout this book and felt affirmed by experiencing some positive outcomes as a result of partnering with your students. You might also have stumbled and perhaps even failed. If you picked yourself up and tried again and again until you improved and perfected a practice, we applaud your effort and determination. It is this type of commitment and willingness to learn through successes and failures that will allow you to continuously learn and lead the effort to finding True North for you and your students. As you read this final chapter, many opportunities will present themselves for you to revisit or extend your learning.

To begin, we will first recap the journey we have traveled throughout this book. We will highlight key concepts and invite you to note ideas and practices you will implement to partner with students to build ownership of learning. Figures 7.1a, 7.1b, and 7.1c provide templates to capture your thoughts and are also available as an electronic version at www.corwin .com/partneringwithstudents.

## RETRACING PART I

**Part I: Defining the Journey** stipulates that the teacher and students must gain clarity on the importance of building collaborative relationships, academic standards, and criteria for success to begin the process of partnering with students. The Teacher's and Learner's Internal Compasses serve as navigational tools to orient teachers and students in the quest for True North: *achieving worthy goals with wisdom and confidence.*

In **Chapter 1**, the emphasis is on creating a collaborative classroom that is learner-centered and learning-focused. The teacher must understand that building relationships with students and among students is essential to establishing the right kind of learning environment for students to flourish and achieve at high levels. The TRUST Model provides a road map to surface beliefs and actions by bringing the voice of the students into the classroom as our partners throughout the teaching and learning process.

Defining what is most important for students to learn first requires the teacher to gain clarity on the scope and depth of any set of academic standards. Teachers must understand the learning progressions and cognitive complexity within the standards in order to plan and assess learning within an appropriate instructional sequence. **Chapter 2** provides the core principles associated with focusing learning that can be translated into clear Learning Intentions for students.

The Handoff described in **Chapter 3** represents the moment when students begin to take ownership of learning and partnering with their teacher and peers. Clear Learning Intentions and co-constructed Success Criteria reveal the entry to the path for students to achieve, broaden, or exceed the Learning Intentions. This not only focuses learning for the teacher and the student, but also paves the way for formative assessment and feedback. As a result, students can begin to craft a response to *What is my contribution? Where am I going? How am I doing?* and *Where to next?*

### Extending Part I

Take time to flip back through the first three chapters and look at any highlighting or notes you may have written. Use the space in Figure 7.1a to jot down your own synthesis of key ideas or practices you want to remember and infuse into your classroom.

**Figure 7.1a**

| PART I: DEFINING THE JOURNEY | KEY IDEAS AND PRACTICES |
|---|---|
| **Chapter 1: *Defining Collaborative Relationships for Learning*** | |
| **Chapter 2: *Defining Essential Learnings*** | |
| **Chapter 3: *Defining Criteria for Success*** | |

## RETRACING PART II

**Part II: Learning on the Journey** requires teachers and students to be strategic and clear on what moves learning forward while immersed in the daily teaching and learning cycle, and what can be transferred to future learning scenarios. It is about building a toolbox of strategies and ways of thinking to reach True North.

**Chapter 4** maintains that the appropriate amount of challenge to assimilate new concepts and skills will directly affect student motivation to learn. The strategies teachers employ to engage and challenge students are only one part of the equation. Students also need multiple Learner Strategies to access when faced with future learning challenges. Partial or Full Transfer from teacher-owned strategies to learner-owned strategies is the ultimate goal.

Feedback nourishes learning through an exchange and is the heart and soul of collaborative partnerships in a classroom. **Chapter 5** asserts that feedback is one of the most critical strategies to be mastered in school and life. The word *feedback* is deconstructed to understand how feedback can accelerate and propel learning forward.

### Extending Part II

Reexamine your notes from Chapters 4 and 5. Use the space in Figure 7.1b to summarize your own ideas and key points you want to remember or consider implementing in your classroom.

**Figure 7.1b**

| PART II: LEARNING ON THE JOURNEY | KEY IDEAS AND PRACTICES |
|---|---|
| **Chapter 4:** *Learner Strategies* | |
| **Chapter 5:** *Learning Through Effective Feedback* | |

## RETRACING PART III

**Part III: Retracing and Extending the Journey** provides the structure for students and teachers to reflect upon what has moved learning forward. This part of the journey requires introspection, analysis, choice, and action for the future on the part of the learner, teacher, and leaders.

In **Chapter 6** teachers work with students to prove their learning as the unit of study culminates. Students provide evidence to demonstrate the achievement of Learning Intentions. They must also analyze the effect of feedback and strategies employed. The information provided by students prompts teachers to reflect on their impact on student learning and Learner Beliefs.

The culminating chapter provides an opportunity to synthesize insights and draft next steps as result of interacting with this book. **Chapter 7** extends an invitation to implement partnering with students beyond a single classroom to sustain the benefits of sharing the ownership of learning school or system-wide. Suggestions are provided for school leaders to lead the adult learning and plan systemic and systematic implementation to build ownership of learning.

### Extending Part III

Review your notes from Chapter 6, using the space in Figure 7.1c to note your own ideas or practices you want to remember that can impact student learning.

Since you have just begun reading Chapter 7, you might elect to use the template in Figure 7.1c as an advance organizer to capture your thoughts as you read through the remainder of the chapter.

**Figure 7.1c**

| PART III: RETRACING AND EXTENDING THE JOURNEY | KEY IDEAS AND PRACTICES |
|---|---|
| **Chapter 6: *Retracing Evidence to Prove and Extend Learning*** | |
| **Chapter 7: *Retracing and Extending the Process: A Summary to Guide Teachers and Leaders*** | |

## RETRACING AND EXTENDING THE COMPASSES

### Heading for True North

The Teacher's and Learner's Internal Compasses are the orienting points to keep you and your students headed in the right direction. Just as explorers can make great headway on any given day and then find the mission stalled, you too will find similar situations with your students. There will certainly be ups and downs. The compasses will keep you grounded in the core concepts and practices as you begin partnering with students to share the responsibility and ownership of learning.

Reread George and Sims's definition of True North from the introduction to this book. Think about your role as the leader and lead learner in the classroom and visualize the Teacher's Internal Compass and the Learner's Internal Compass:

True North is the internal compass that guides you successfully through life. It represents who you are as a human being at your deepest level. It is your orienting point—your fixed point in a spinning world—that helps you stay on track as a leader. Your True North is based on what is most important to you, your most cherished values, your passions and motivations, the sources of satisfaction in your life. (George & Sims, 2007, p. xxiii)

### Retracing and Extending the Teacher's Internal Compass

As you chew on the meaning of True North, what is the internal compass that orients you each and every day as you work with students? Pause to think deeply about what you value, about the moments that give you joy and satisfaction, about your decision to become a teacher. What brings you back to the classroom day after day and year after year? Use Figure 7.2 to engage in the following exercises designed to synthesize the foundational practices and personalize your True North. You will also find an electronic version of the compass at www.corwin.com/partneringwithstudents.

- In the center of the compass, compose your own statement to capture what orients you to your purpose and calling, your True North.
- Once you are clear on your purpose, look at each cardinal point. As you read through each foundational practice to partnering with students, create a "word splash" of as many words or phrases as you associate with this practice. An example has been provided for the first cardinal point, North.

**Figure 7.2**  Teacher's Internal Compass Personalized

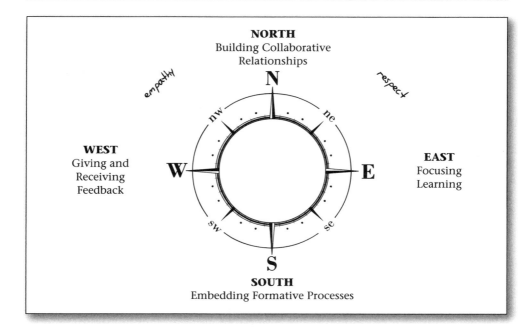

## Retracing and Extending the Learner's Internal Compass

*You have brains in your head. You have feet in your shoes. You can steer yourself any direction you choose.*

—Dr. Seuss, *Oh, the Places You Will Go!*

It is unlikely that you will hear students ask any of the questions surrounding the Learner's Internal Compass. You will most likely need to interpret their questions and statements to determine how they are progressing in their learning as well as their receptiveness to owning the learning. For example, imagine a student saying, "This is dumb! Why are we doing this?" Some may conclude that the student is unmotivated, or even that the lesson is not well designed. However, with a little probing we can get to the real reason behind this simple question and might discover that the Learning Intention and purpose of the lesson are unclear, or that the student doesn't see the connection to the Success Criteria. This simple statement cues us to two things. First, the student is asking, *Where am I going?* Second, the teacher can begin to generate a series of responses based upon the student's questions that may include, "I need to think about focusing learning. Did I miss a step?"

Learning to listen to students and decode the meaning behind their questions or comments can cue you to what they need. It also provides an opportunity to reflect upon your practices to guide appropriate actions. Use the Learner's Internal Compass in Figure 7.3 (see p. 148) to try one of the following exercises:

- Access an electronic copy of the Figure 7.3 template and make a point to *listen carefully* to your students' comments. Jot down the students' questions or statements to categorize their comments by the appropriate cardinal point.
- From memory, generate as many questions or statements as you have heard from students that cue you to the cardinal questions. A few examples have been created to help you get started.

An electronic version of the template is available at www.corwin.com/partneringwithstudents.

## Retracing and Extending the Compasses—the Alignment

There is a powerful and reciprocal relationship between the Teacher's and Learner's Internal Compasses. One cannot exist or thrive without the other! In Figure 7.4 (see page 149), we overlay the two compasses to reveal how they are explicitly connected to form a united vision of True North. The

**Figure 7.3**  Learner's Internal Compass Personalized

NORTH
What is my contribution?
*I would really like to work with Miguel. He helps me focus.*

**N**

*nw* · · · *ne*

WEST
Where to next?
*What do I need to do*
*to get a new job?*

**W**                                    **E**

EAST
Where am I going?
*I need to learn these*
*math facts to stop*
*making simple errors.*

*sw* · · · *se*

**S**

SOUTH
How am I doing
*Is this correct?*

teacher's foundational practice, such as Building Collaborative Relationships, can be viewed as the impetus behind learner questions such as *Do I matter?* implying *What is my contribution?* We can also think of the teacher practices as a direct response to learners' inquiries during the teaching and learning process. For example, a student might voice something akin to *I think I've got it—can you check my work?* implying *Where to next?* The teacher can respond with meaningful feedback and the student's own evidence of progress toward meeting the Learning Intentions. Why is this relationship so critical? Because it moves learning forward in powerful ways.

The cardinal points on the Teacher's Internal Compass capture foundational practices that have been extensively studied and shown to nearly double the rate of learning (Black & Wiliam, 1998; Cornelius-White & Harbaugh, 2010; Hattie, 2009, 2012; Wiliam, 2011). However, when students are guided to own the learning, and confidently respond to *Where am I going? How am I doing?* and *Where to next?* the rate of learning can triple (Hattie, 2009, 2012). Imagine the power of integrating these practices!

It is our belief that when teachers and students move fluently between the Teacher's and Learner's Internal Compasses, learning becomes highly visible and transparent to the teacher and the learner. Once again, it is worth repeating John Hattie's description of Visible Learning: "When teachers see learning through the eyes of the student and students see themselves as their own teachers" (Hattie, 2013, p. 25). The Teacher's and Learner's Internal Compasses provide the orientation and the navigational tools to make the trek to finding True North highly visible.

**Figure 7.4** Teacher's and Learner's Internal Compasses Aligned

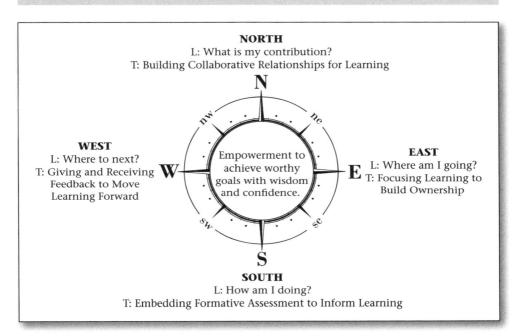

**NORTH**
L: What is my contribution?
T: Building Collaborative Relationships for Learning

**WEST**
L: Where to next?
T: Giving and Receiving Feedback to Move Learning Forward

Empowerment to achieve worthy goals with wisdom and confidence.

**EAST**
L: Where am I going?
T: Focusing Learning to Build Ownership

**SOUTH**
L: How am I doing?
T: Embedding Formative Assessment to Inform Learning

## Teacher's Internal Compass: Taking Action

As a teacher embarking on this journey, we hope you see yourself as an explorer flanked by a team of students and, hopefully, supportive colleagues. You are taking the necessary steps to make learning visible and transparent for you and your students. You are the brave adventurer willing to see students as partners and ready to take on the challenge. Be a risk-taker. Plan your journey, prepare for many challenges and setbacks, be willing to make midcourse corrections and set sail!

We know our mission is to empower all learners with the wisdom and confidence to exceed expectations. So where do we begin? Let's begin with our beliefs. We encourage you to intentionally reflect on your current practices and the changes you would like to make, related to each cardinal point on the compass. Figure 7.5 offers a template for taking action, which you will also find at www.corwin.com/partneringwithstudents.

**Figure 7.5**  The Teacher's Internal Compass: Getting Ready to Take Action

| Cardinal Points | Reflection Questions | Actions I Will Take |
|---|---|---|
| **North: *Building Relationships*** | ❏ Have I been successful in the past building trusting relationships with my students?<br>❏ In my classroom, is there a culture of responsive and respectful interaction and speech among all members?<br>❏ Do my students believe they are critical members of the learning team?<br>❏ Have I built structures for collaboration and student leadership?<br>❏ Did I take the time to work on building collaborative relationships throughout the year?<br>❏ Are my students able to answer *What is my contribution?* | |
| **East: *Focusing Learning*** | ❏ Do I understand the progression of learning required of students within the academic standards?<br>❏ Have I translated learning for students into meaningful Learning Intentions and Success Criteria?<br>❏ Have I focused learning to the point that all of my students are able to articulate *Where am I going? How am I doing?* and *Where to next?* | |
| **South: *Embedding Formative Processes*** | ❏ Do students in my classroom have their own strategies for learning?<br>❏ Do I use feedback from students to change my instruction?<br>❏ Do students know if they are making progress and what they need to do next?<br>❏ Do they know and have proof to demonstrate the achievement of the Learning Intentions? | |
| **West: *Giving and Receiving Feedback*** | ❏ Have I established effective feedback practices in my classroom to give and receive feedback from students?<br>❏ Do students engage in giving and receiving feedback from one another (teacher, self, peer)? | |

# EXTENDING THE JOURNEY: THE ROLE OF SCHOOL LEADERS

*No leader single-handedly ever gets anything extraordinary done.*

—James M. Kouzes and Barry Z. Posner,
*Turning Adversity Into Opportunity*

With such an important journey ahead of you, we return to the idea of assembling a team. In the introduction, we shared that the early explorers in search of True North did so with a strong leader, a group of skilled and purpose-driven partners, and much planning and determination. We believe this journey will require the same effort.

This book has focused on how teachers partner with students to build ownership of learning. The learning benefits for the teacher and the student are immense. And yet it can all end on the last day of school. It is highly unlikely that the students will rise up and demand to be viewed as partners should the next teacher operate in a traditional manner. Students' voices will not be solicited, and within a very short amount of time they will easily slip back into old habits and perhaps remember fondly the one year they were energized and fully engaged in learning.

As a leader, we challenge you to consider how you might partner with teachers and other leaders within your school or district to change your story. What would this look like? How can leaders partner with teachers or other leaders to ensure that students are at the center of learning and have an authentic voice? Before we offer suggestions on how to begin the partnership with teachers, we will touch upon the current research and suggest you examine your own beliefs as a leader.

## Leadership That Counts: What We Know

There are literally thousands of books, degree programs, seminars, and even life coaches who can offer their spin on what it means to be an effective leader in schools. We can even visit schools where inspired leadership has turned a dismal and failing school into a place of wonder and see dedicated teachers and students continually exceed expectations. What is the recipe for success? After conducting over 800 meta-analyses, Hattie concluded in *Visible Learning for Teachers*, "There is no recipe for success, no professional development set of worksheets, no new teaching method, and no band-aid remedy. It is a way of thinking. But there are practices we know are effective and many practices that we know are not" (2012, pp. 22–23).

According to the current research on leadership, the fundamental role of any leader in schools today is to be the *lead learner* and to *lead learning*

(Robinson, 2011). Vivian Robinson maintains that leadership can be shared or distributed, and as a result there can be many leaders in a school. A principal, headmaster, dean, department chair, or team leader all have varying degrees of formal authority, while other staff members might exercise leadership through their expertise, principles, or personal attributes. The school leader is key and absolutely essential to implementing systemic and systematic changes in a school to benefit *all* students by tapping into the strengths of all.

Robinson encourages us to shift our thinking from describing leadership as a *style* (i.e., instructional or transformational leadership) to thinking about leadership *practices* that are associated with higher levels of student achievement. After reviewing thousands of studies on leadership, Robinson found only thirty studies linking leadership to student achievement. She discovered the highest effect of leadership on student learning occurred when leaders were intimately involved in *leading teacher learning and development*. Student achievement gains more than doubled when associated with this one variable. It must be noted that there are four other interrelated leadership practices that surfaced in the research, but none as striking as this one. For more information, we encourage our readers to access the Best Evidence Synthesis at www.corwin.com/partneringwithstudents.

As a leader you might feel a bit intimidated and think, "How am I to lead teacher learning and development when I am just beginning to grasp the concept of partnering with students to build ownership of learning myself?" As the leader of the school, you are not expected to be the expert; nor are you expected to fully understand the depth and breadth of partnering with students. Instead, your role is to learn and lead the vision and plans to initiate and support the implementation process. Just as we want teachers to learn alongside their students, you too will learn alongside the staff. Just as we want teachers to observe and listen closely to their students to determine next steps, you too will observe and listen to teachers *and* students, to determine next steps. However, before you launch the journey, we invite you to examine your leadership beliefs and purpose.

### Leading Change: Extending the Partnership

> *Just as a compass points toward a magnetic field, your True North pulls you toward the purpose of your leadership. When you follow your internal compass, your leadership will be authentic. . . .*
>
> —Bill George and Peter Sims, *True North: Discover Your Authentic Leadership*

We encourage you, as the leader, to engage in an internal dialogue to surface why you are in a position of leadership. What brings you satisfaction in a position that has many competing demands and incredible stress? What are your aspirations, hopes, and dreams for the students and teachers looking to you for guidance? In short, what is your purpose?

We encourage you to pause at this time and think deeply to construct your True North statement using the Leader's Internal Compass in Figure 7.6. What are the critical cardinal points or essential leadership practices you believe help orient you toward True North? As you engage in this exercise, draw upon all of your experiences and knowledge as a leader. You will notice that the learner (L) and teacher (T) cardinal points are included so you can consider how your compass points align. An electronic version is also available at www.corwin.com/partneringwithstudents.

**Figure 7.6**  Leader's Internal Compass: True North

**NORTH**
Leader: _____
L: What is my contribution?
T: Building Collaborative Relationships for Learning

**WEST**
Leader: _____
L: Where to next?
T: Giving and Receiving
Feedback to Move
Learning Forward

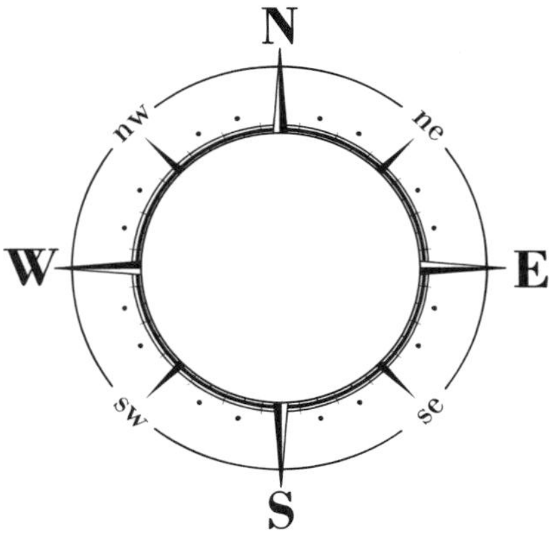

**EAST**
Leader: _____
L: Where am I going?
T: Focusing Learning to
Build Ownership

**SOUTH**
Leader: _____
L: How am I doing?
T: Embedding Formative Assessment to Inform Learning

## The Partnership: Building Trust

The relationships built within the walls of a school will determine whether change will or will not occur. How will you partner with your staff? Teachers need to trust their leaders to be transparent, open, honest, fair, and *kind*. Just like students, teachers need some "wiggle room" to take risks, stumble, fall, fail, and finally succeed in order to learn and grow their Talent. Promoting and fostering collaborative relationships with staff and among staff members is a critical first step. Although it is beyond the scope of this book, we hope you will also consider how to extend the partnership to involve parents and other significant adults who influence students' beliefs about learning. By considering all the stakeholders, the desired outcome of partnering with students to build ownership of learning will have broad-based support.

The TRUST Model described in Chapter 1 is a meaningful way to explore partnering within the school. The framework establishes key factors in building collaborative relationships and offers a way to begin planning meaningful interactions to build a learning community. Figure 7.7 provides a place to review and apply the TRUST Model in a schoolwide setting. Use the reflection questions to think about the staff's current status and needs, as well as possible actions you might consider now and throughout the implementation phase. An electronic version is available at www.corwin.com/partneringwithstudents.

## Defining the Journey: Leading the Inquiry

*School improvement should not be seen as a one-time event. It is a marathon, or perhaps a series of marathons, not a 100-meter dash.*

—B. R. Jones, *Imperative Leadership:*
*What Must Be Done for Students to Succeed*

When thinking about how to move adult learning forward, two key factors should be considered. First: How receptive is the staff to the idea of partnering with students to share the ownership of learning? Where are we in the process of partnering with students? How many of the components of the process are in place in the school, and in how many classrooms? Second: What might be a good starting place for the staff? How can we map the journey from our current state to the desired state?

We suggest building a shared knowledge base regarding the elements essential to partnering with students to build ownership of learning. You might begin by reading the book with your building leadership team or perhaps with other school leaders. However, at some point you will want to engage the entire staff in deep learning to begin partnering with students. A schoolwide book study is a good place to start building a shared understanding, a common language, and potential outcomes that would indicate the criteria for success.

**Figure 7.7** Leaders' TRUST Model for Planning: Building Collaborative Relationships

| TRUST Model for Leaders | Reflection Questions | Actions I Will Take |
|---|---|---|
| **Talent**<br><br>Deliberate actions to discover and develop the *talent and beliefs* all staff members bring to the classroom or school. | ❏ How do I optimize and grow the talents and abilities of the staff for the purpose of building ownership of learning in students? | |
| **Rapport + Responsiveness**<br><br>The ability to build relationships of trust and mutual respect and to respond or react appropriately to support to each staff member. | ❏ How do I engage each person to be a proactive member of our school community? | |
| **"Us" Factor**<br><br>A shared belief that everyone can learn and everyone is a vital contributor to the learning process. | ❏ How do I develop a school-wide plan of action team that includes all voices focused on adult and student learning? | |
| **Structures**<br><br>The methods, procedures, and practices that will enable staff to become partners in the learning process and to own the schoolwide action plan. | ❏ What structures will support the staff to effectively work and learn together as a team as we plan and begin the implementation process? | |
| **Time**<br><br>The requirement of purposeful and intentional time dedicated to building collaborative relationships and developing beliefs and action plans. | ❏ What time can I carve out to build collaborative relationships and support teams to achieve our goals? | |

You will find many resources in this book and on our website to help build a common knowledge base within any group. Use your professional judgment to determine how to use the Book Study Guide at the end of the book, as well as the Time for Application exercises and Summing Up sections embedded in the chapters. As authors and veteran consultants, we are also available to provide professional development sessions to introduce and deepen the understanding of the core concepts of partnering with students.

The template in Figure 7.8 can have many applications as you begin to learn and also lead the learning to understand the implications of partnering with students. For example, after reading Part I, Chapters 1–3, you might ask the group to synthesize the key points and begin drafting ideas to make visible the criteria that would be common in the school across all grade levels or content areas. The conversation needs to focus on what teachers will be doing, but even more important, on how to include the voice of students. Examining the criteria for success from the perspective of what we will hear and see from our students provides the much-needed "reality check" missing from most of our school improvement efforts. This is a critical element to seeing students as our partners in learning.

The initial conversations and deep thinking about the key ideas, practices, and criteria for success will provide the backbone to plan for deep implementation. This simple template can be used as your GPS to plan and monitor the initial learning and also the deep implementation effort to follow. You will undoubtedly encounter detours and roadblocks that will require some rethinking and adjustments. After all, you are leading the journey, an exciting expedition into new territory. Every expedition must be prepared to use the best available data and information at hand to make midcourse corrections. Expedition leaders rely on the team while providing clear leadership around the shared vision of finding True North together.

### Learning on the Journey: Providing Effective Feedback

Once you begin to craft the criteria for success, there will be adventurous teachers who will be chomping at the bit to try the ideas. These brave teachers will experiment, learn from mistakes, and help pave the way for others. However, they will also need your support and encouragement to be risk-takers. The feedback you provide can do much to encourage their efforts while also providing valuable information to address during the implementation phase.

Chapter 5 establishes the importance of providing effective feedback to move learning forward. The question for leaders is whether or not the components of effective feedback are in place within the school for adult and student learners. As you consider the plans you have crafted up to this point, how can feedback be used to promote teacher learning and your own learning as the leader? Use Figure 7.9 to review and develop plans around the components of effective feedback. The template is also available as an electronic version at www.corwin.com/partneringwithstudents.

**Figure 7.8** Partnering With Students to Build Ownership of Learning: Planning Template

| PART I: DEFINING THE JOURNEY | KEY IDEAS AND PRACTICES | Criteria for Success: What Will It Look Like in Our Classrooms? | Criteria for Success: What Will We See and Hear From Our Students? |
|---|---|---|---|
| **Chapter 1:** *Defining Collaborative Relationships for Learning* | | | |
| **Chapter 2:** *Defining Essential Learnings* | | | |
| **Chapter 3:** *Defining Criteria for Success* | | | |
| PART II: LEARNING ON THE JOURNEY | KEY IDEAS AND PRACTICES | Criteria for Success: What Will It Look Like in Our Classrooms? | Criteria for Success: What Will We See and Hear From Our Students? |
| **Chapter 4:** *Learner Strategies for Life* | | | |
| **Chapter 5:** *Learning Through Effective Feedback* | | | |
| PART III: RETRACING AND EXTENDING THE JOURNEY | KEY IDEAS AND PRACTICES | Criteria for Success: What Will It Look Like in Our Classrooms? | Criteria for Success: What Will We See and Hear From Our Students? |
| **Chapter 6:** *Retracing Evidence to Prove and Extend Learning* | | | |
| **Chapter 7:** *Retracing and Extending the Process: A Summary to Guide Teachers and Leaders* | | | |

**Figure 7.9** Effective Feedback for Adult Learners

| Provide Effective Feedback | Reflection Questions | Actions |
|---|---|---|
| **F**REQUENT—Feedback is intentional and responsive to the teacher's need for immediate or delayed feedback. | ❐ How often should feedback be given, based on progression of adult learning? | |
| **E**FFICACIOUS—Feedback is focused on progress, not the person, and is given to review, reflect upon, and make changes. | ❐ How do we work to focus feedback on progress, rather than on proficiency or personality? | |
| **EX**CHANGE-ORIENTED—The exchange of feedback is modeled, and adults have been provided with structures that allow them to be part of the exchange. | ❐ How to do I put structures in place to ensure effective feedback among adult learners? | |
| **D**IFFERENTIATED—Feedback is personalized and aligned to the needs of each learner. | ❐ How do we ensure that feedback is personalized for each teacher and leader? | |
| **B**ALANCED—Feedback is balanced between self, peer, and leader. | ❐ How often do we self- and peer-assess to provide additional feedback? | |
| **A**CCURATE—Feedback is targeted at a level most appropriate for each learner and works to deepen learning. | ❐ How do we ensure that the feedback given to teachers and leaders is accurate to their learning needs? | |
| **C**RITERIA-DRIVEN—Feedback is based on the Success Criteria to ensure a clear understanding of what is expected. | ❐ What criteria is used to provide feedback? | |
| **K**INESTHETIC—The elements of the TRUST Model establish the right environment for feedback to be received and acted upon. | ❐ Is the feedback being received and acted upon? How do I know? | |

## Retracing and Extending the Journey: *Building for Success*

Will the change we plan so carefully last? In order to ensure that the process of partnering with students to build ownership of learning gains momentum, we must ensure that reflection and celebration are a part of the journey. How do we know that what we are doing is working, and how does that inform our next steps? What is the body of evidence that supports the practices and strategies that have become commonplace?

Just as students create a learning portfolio, we suggest adults do the same. We encourage you to compile evidence from the learning that has taken place at your school. Take time to align that evidence to the Success Criteria and goals established by your staff in the schoolwide action plan. A portfolio can be created and shared electronically in a collection of documents or in a slide show. Even a bulletin board complete with pictures, testimonials, and other artifacts can be used to share your journey. These artifacts will give rise to authentic celebration of success and open the door to meaningful discussion that may provide great insights. It will propel discussion forward to guide next steps in the learning process for adults.

Taking the time to partner with your staff may not be an easy road or one that is well traveled, but it will result in meaningful change and deepened collaboration and ultimately empower students. We encourage you to be a learner of this process as a leader and to be willing to take on the challenge, make mistakes, get up and try again tomorrow, and make it happen in your school.

## SUMMING UP: STUDENTS AS OUR GREATEST ASSETS

*If students are going to be our partners in the classrooms and the corridors of our schools, we need to speak a common language.*

—Russell Quaglia, keynote address,
Corwin authors' retreat, 2014

As we bring this book to a close, we want to focus attention on the greatest asset in the schools—*our students*. Have we really unlocked their potential? Are they aware of their own potential? Are they truly our partners in learning?

Students will not happen upon the changes outlined in this book without you. For years, they have been taught the game of school and are well versed in the current rules. *Change the rules!* Perhaps include student representatives in the book study, professional development, and planning for implementation. Their voices can only inform and enrich the work. Allow students to be fully vested and engaged partners.

What do we want to achieve? In the end, we hope to *empower students as owners of learning as they strive to reach and exceed worthy goals in their lives.* We also know that in order for students to see themselves differently, as owners of learning, we must see them differently. It is not only our job to help students find their True North; it is our *imperative*. The world today needs students ready to take on worthy and challenging goals, to fail, to get up, to fail again, and to persist until their goals are realized. We need students who see challenge as an invitation, rather than as an impassible roadblock. *We need difference makers, legacy builders, and world changers. We can be that for them so that they can be that for others.*

# Study Guide

## PART I: DEFINING THE JOURNEY

We hope you have learned much from reading this book and that you and your colleagues will engage in deep and long-lasting learning around partnering with students to build ownership of learning. The book study section is set up in a simple but meaningful format to foster conversation, decision-making, and implementation of the ideas presented in this book—and, more important, the ideas generated at your school.

After reading each chapter, begin by focusing the conversation around the essential questions found at the beginning and end of each chapter. You may also refer to the discussion topics listed to generate discussion. Next, brainstorm ideas about what is already taking place and what could change, and make a plan to get started. Each chapter offers many ideas for implementation in the sections marked *Time for Application*. Use these sections as a starting place to generate and discuss ideas. Include your own ideas and best practices to build a plan. Finally, make time to check in and make midcourse adjustments, determine progress, and plan next steps together.

The following templates are referenced in Chapter 7 and are also available to use as part of a book study. You may access the electronic templates at www.corwin.com/partneringwithstudents.

Figures 7.1a–7.1c: Defining the Journey, Learning on the Journey, and Retracing and Extending the Journey

Figure 7.8: Partnering With Students to Build Ownership of Learning

## Introduction: Finding True North: A Compass for Teaching and Learning, and Chapter 1: Defining Collaborative Relationships for Learning

### Essential Questions

- How can relationships impede or catapult learning?
- How do I establish a classroom where learning is a partnership?
- How do I find clarity in a sea of standards?

### Discussion Topics

- Student voice
- Collaborative student–teacher relationships
- Teacher's and Learner's Internal Compasses
- The TRUST Model

### Ideas for Interacting With the Content: Time for Application

- Which ideas from the *Time for Application* section of the chapter were particularly appealing and worth trying?
- What are we already doing?
- What might we be able to implement right away?
- What are some of our long-term goals for implementation?
- What steps will we take to get started?
- How will we monitor and grow our learning over time?

### Next Steps

✓ When will we check in and discuss progress?
✓ How will we know if we are successful?

## Chapter 2: Defining Essential Learnings

### Essential Questions

- How do I find clarity in a sea of standards?

### Discussion Topics

- Identifying the learning progressions
- Developing an instructional sequence

### Ideas for Interacting With the Content: Time for Application

- Which ideas from the *Time for Application* section of the chapter were particularly appealing and worth trying?
- What are we already doing?

- What might we be able to implement right away?
- What are some of our long-term goals for implementation?
- What steps will we take to get started?
- How will we monitor and grow our learning over time?

### Next Steps

✓ When will we check in and discuss progress?
✓ How will we know if we are successful?

## Chapter 3: Defining Criteria for Success

### Essential Questions

- How can teachers translate standards into criteria for success?
- How can students develop personalized learning goals?
- How do we put beliefs about learning into action?

### Discussion Topics

- The Handoff
- Co-constructing Success Criteria

### Ideas for Interacting With the Content: Time for Application

- Which ideas from the *Time for Application* section of the chapter were particularly appealing and worth trying?
- What are we already doing?
- What might we be able to implement right away?
- What are some of our long-term goals for implementation?
- What steps will we take to get started?
- How will we monitor and grow our learning over time?

### Next Steps

✓ When will we check in and discuss progress?
✓ How will we know if we are successful?

# PART II: LEARNING ON THE JOURNEY

## Chapter 4: Learner Strategies for Life

### Essential Questions

- How do teachers support students in developing strategies for learning?

*Discussion Topics*

- Defining and developing Learner Strategies
- Full versus Partial Transfer
- The learning portfolio

*Ideas for Interacting With the Content: Time for Application*

- Which ideas from the *Time for Application* section of the chapter were particularly appealing and worth trying?
- What are we already doing?
- What might we be able to implement right away?
- What are some of our long-term goals for implementation?
- What steps will we take to get started?
- How will we monitor and grow our learning over time?

*Next Steps*

- ✓ When will we check in and discuss progress?
- ✓ How will we know if we are successful?

## Chapter 5: Learning Through Effective Feedback

*Essential Questions*

- How can feedback propel learning forward for teachers and students?

*Discussion Topics*

- Nourishing learning
- The FEEDBACK acronym

*Ideas for Interacting With the Content: Time for Application*

- Which ideas from the *Time for Application* section of the chapter were particularly appealing and worth trying?
- What are we already doing?
- What might we be able to implement right away?
- What are some of our long-term goals for implementation?
- What steps will we take to get started?
- How will we monitor and grow our learning over time?

*Next Steps*

- ✓ When will we check in and discuss progress?
- ✓ How will we know if we are successful?

# PART III: RETRACING AND EXTENDING THE JOURNEY

## Chapter 6: Retracing Evidence to Prove and Extend Learning

### Essential Questions

- How can students and teachers prove deep learning has occurred?
- How can proving Learner Strategies lead to deepened ownership of learning?

### Discussion Topics

- Retracing and proving learning with evidence
- The learning portfolio

### Ideas for Interacting With the Content: Time for Application

- Which ideas from the *Time for Application* section of the chapter were particularly appealing and worth trying?
- What are we already doing?
- What might we be able to implement right away?
- What are some of our long-term goals for implementation?
- What steps will we take to get started?
- How will we monitor and grow our learning over time?

### Next Steps

✓ When will we check in and discuss progress?
✓ How will we know if we are successful?

## Chapter 7: Retracing and Extending the Process: A Summary to Guide Teachers and Leaders

### Essential Questions

- How can I leverage the strengths of all to take action?
- How can the compasses guide collective action?

### Discussion Topics

- Retracing and extending key ideas and practices presented in the book
- Teacher leadership
- School leadership
- Students as greatest assets

### *Ideas for Interacting With the Content: Time for Application*

- Which ideas from the *Time for Application* section of the chapter were particularly appealing and worth trying?
- What are we already doing?
- What might we be able to implement right away?
- What are some of our long-term goals for implementation?
- What steps will we take to get started?
- How will we monitor and grow our learning over time?

### *Next Steps*

✓ When will we check in and discuss progress?
✓ How will we know if we are successful?

# Appendices

Appendices A–E provide three distinct examples of belief systems around learning. The first are the CA²RE beliefs, which offer one way to categorize the beliefs of learners, teachers, and leaders. The second example is from Stonefields School in Auckland, New Zealand, and provides a student-friendly example of beliefs and values in addition to the example offered in Chapter 1. The third is from Ricardo Flores Magon Academy in Denver, Colorado, and includes its credos and values.

Appendices F and G provide examples of science and math learning progressions. Finally, Appendix H provides a classroom example of co-constructed Success Criteria from Tara Lindburg of Academy Charter School in Castle Rock, Colorado.

## APPENDIX A

| CA²RE Learner Beliefs and Practices | |
|---|---|
| **Role** | **Practices** |
| The **C**ommunicator | ☐ My classroom conversations are focused on learning.<br>☐ I share strategies that work for me with peers.<br>☐ Talking with others helps me clarify my thinking and learning. |
| The **A**ppraiser | ☐ I seek evidence to determine if I am reaching my learning goals.<br>☐ I see the work and tests in my class as information to me about what I have and have not yet learned.<br>☐ I think about which strategies work for me and try them in new situations. |
| The **A**ctivator | ☐ I know that if I didn't learn it today, I can try a new method tomorrow.<br>☐ I know that learning is hard work and takes perseverance.<br>☐ When I struggle through problems, I am becoming a more skillful learner. |
| The **R**elationship Builder | ☐ I trust myself, my peers, and my teacher as teammates to help me learn.<br>☐ I care about others and treat everyone respectfully.<br>☐ I know it is important to understand many points of view to broaden my understanding of diverse opinions and beliefs. |
| The **E**ngager | ☐ I listen to others because I know we can learn from one another.<br>☐ I enjoy challenge and persist to find solutions to the problems by myself or with others.<br>☐ I set and strive to achieve challenging and worthwhile goals. |

# APPENDIX B

| CA$^2$RE Teacher Beliefs and Practices | |
|---|---|
| **Role** | **Practices** |
| The **C**ommunicator | ❐ When talking with others, I usually describe what students are learning more than a strategy I used.<br>❐ I spend less time talking and more time listening to students' discussions with peers to determine next steps that will accelerate learning.<br>❐ I know that when students engage in dialogue with one another, they deepen their thinking and learn to appreciate different points of view and how to resolve conflict. |
| The **A**ppraiser | ❐ I assess students to determine which students I taught well and those I did not teach as effectively.<br>❐ I observe and listen intently to what students are saying to one another and to me to determine errors, misconceptions, and success.<br>❐ I use evidence from multiple sources to determine my next steps. |
| The **A**ctivator | ❐ I actively model metacognitive strategies to demonstrate how to welcome mistakes as opportunities to learn.<br>❐ When students succeed or fail, I initiate an internal conversation about what I did or did not do.<br>❐ My role is to stimulate change in each student to close the gap between what is known and unknown. |
| The **R**elationship Builder | ❐ I create a safe learning environment that is characterized by trust, warmth, empathy, and positive relationships with my students.<br>❐ I work to create a community of learners who trust one another, understand that each person plays a critical role in learning, and are willing to take risks.<br>❐ My classroom is a safe haven where students learn to trust me and one another so they can freely make mistakes, ask for help, and learn to be risk-takers for the sake of learning. |
| The **E**ngager | ❐ I enjoy the challenge of teaching and learning and strive to impart the desire to excel to my students through my words and actions.<br>❐ I engage students in meaningful challenges that require persistence, concentration, and practice.<br>❐ I know we are deeply engaged in learning when my head and students' heads hurt from thinking. |

## APPENDIX C

| CA²RE Leader Beliefs and Practices | | |
|---|---|---|
| **Role** | **Practices** | |
| | *My Direct Impact on Teachers* | *My Indirect Impact on Students* |
| The **C**ommunicator | ❐ I confer with teachers to talk about how their learning is affecting the learning of the students.<br>❐ We talk about the research on learning and how to implement best practices with fidelity.<br>❐ Teachers explore their effects on students and thrive on feedback as a way to continually improve. | ❐ I observe teachers listening to and watching their students to determine the impact of their teaching to plan next steps.<br>❐ Students are able to talk about errors or mistakes and Learner Strategies that worked or didn't work.<br>❐ Teachers model metacognitive strategies and listen to students explain their thinking. |
| The **A**ppraiser | ❐ I use agreed-upon observational protocols to determine the level of implementation and effectiveness of our improvement goals to guide next steps.<br>❐ I seek evidence to evaluate the effect of my leadership practices on improving the quality of teaching to increase student learning. | ❐ I use anecdotal observational data and a variety of student assessment data to compare the data collected with expected achievement levels.<br>❐ I seek multiple sources of evidence to evaluate student learning as a result of improved teaching. |
| The **A**ctivator | ❐ Improvement of teaching quality and success of teachers is about what I did or did not do.<br>❐ I understand that leading the work with teachers requires persistence, concentration, practice, and struggle. | ❐ The failure or success of students is a result of what I did or did not do to ensure the success of teachers acting on their learning.<br>❐ Seeing students and teachers working equally hard at learning and teaching tells me I'm doing something right. |

| CA²RE Leader Beliefs and Practices | | |
|---|---|---|
| **Role** | **Practices** | |
| | *My Direct Impact on Teachers* | *My Indirect Impact on Students* |
| The **R**elationship Builder | ❒ My role is to develop relationships with all stakeholders. A culture of trust, mutual respect, and honesty creates an environment that supports the learning of adults. | ❒ Students are direct beneficiaries of our culture. Teachers form positive relationships with students that encourage risk-taking and acceptance of mistakes. |
| The **E**ngager | ❒ Teachers do most of the analysis and talking about their learning in staff meetings, professional learning, or coaching sessions.<br>❒ I am never satisfied with just doing my best. Teachers deserve more from leaders, and will respond to high expectations. | ❒ I observe teachers listening to and observing their students to determine the impact of their teaching to plan next steps.<br>❒ Students respond to high expectations from leaders and teachers; they set and achieve challenging and meaningful learning goals. |

## APPENDIX D

### Stonefields School: Values and Beliefs

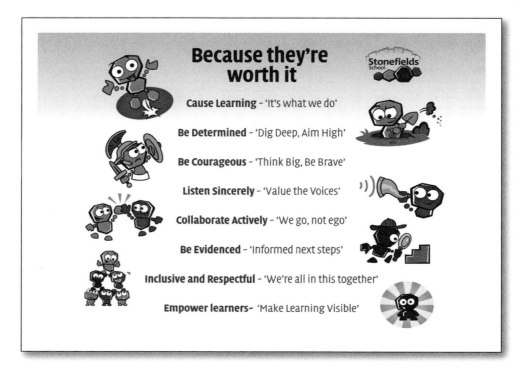

### Stonefields School Learner Dispositions

# APPENDIX E

## Ricardo Flores Magon K–8 Academy, Credos and Values

*What Is a Magonista?*

---

### Credos

Magonistas are taught right, therefore they must act right.
Dialogue is a prerequisite for peace.
If there is injustice, Magonistas listen and speak out.
If Magonistas choose it, another world is possible.
Magonista choices are just choices and just choices build a just society.

---

## VALUES

### Dignified/Dignos

Magonistas act with self-respect and respect others. They act with integrity and know that they will do what is right, regardless of the circumstances; they seek and speak the truth.

*Dignified Magonistas fly high above the negativity; the racism, classism, and prejudice that exist on the ground below. They do not allow the things that happen in their lives keep them from rising up and knowing they are as valuable as anyone else.*

### United/Unidos

Magonistas will work together to meet their collective social, intellectual, and cultural goals. They understand that they are a part of a community and they work to educate and create a more just society.

*Magonistas always work together with their compañeros. Magonistas cooperate to make the world better. They take care of each other and help each other to make good decisions.*

### Problem Solvers/Solucionistas

Magonistas use their logic and reasoning skills to solve all problems in a thorough and peaceful manner to create positive change.

*Magonistas see problems as puzzles that need to be solved. They work to find the answers for their questions. They do not complain about problems, they find solutions to problems.*

### Humble/Humildes

Magonistas are willing to listen and understand that another's reasonable opinions or views deserve respect. Magonistas are generous and they always value their roots. They are confident in their abilities and in the beauty of their community, but they are never arrogant.

*Magonistas ALWAYS remember their roots. They can be dignified but never arrogant. Magonistas understand that even the tallest tree only exists because of the soil, water, and sunlight; the people who helped them along the way and their culture and families. They treat others the way they would want to be treated.*

### Diligent/Diligentes

Magonistas always give the maximum effort in anything they do. They never leave a task unfinished and always take ownership of an issue.

*Magonistas work hard and do what they are required without being asked. They always take responsibility for their actions. They finish what they start and always try their hardest.*

# APPENDIX F

## High School Science Learning Progression Example

|  | Webb's Depth of Knowledge (DOK) |
|---|---|
| Level 1 | Recall and Reproduction |
| Descriptor | Recall of a fact, information, or procedure |
| Level 2 | Skills and Concepts |
| Descriptor | Use of information, conceptual knowledge, procedures, two or more steps, etc. |
| Level 3 | Short-Term Strategic Thinking |
| Descriptor | Requires reasoning, developing a plan or sequence of steps; has some complexity; more than one possible answer |
| Level 4 | Extended Thinking |
| Descriptor | Requires an investigation; time to think and process multiple conditions of the problem or task |

*Source:* "Alignment, Depth of Knowledge, and Change," by N. L. Webb, Wisconsin Center for Education Research, 2005. Florida Educational Research Association fiftieth annual meeting, November 17, 2005. Retrieved from http://facstaff.wcer.wisc.edu/normw/

## SCIENCE SAMPLE

### New Generation Science Standards, High School, Energy (2013)

HS-PS3–1: Create a computational model to calculate the change in energy of one component in a system when the change in energy of the other component(s) and energy flows in and out of the system are known.

HS-PS3–2: Develop and use models to illustrate that energy at the macroscopic scale can be accounted for as a combination of energy associated with the motions of particles (objects) and energy associated with the relative position of particles (objects).

HS-PS3–3: Design, build, and refine a device that works within given constraints to convert one form of energy into another form of energy.

HS-PS3–4: Plan and conduct an investigation to provide evidence that the transfer of thermal energy when two components of different temperature are combined within a closed system results in a more uniform energy distribution among the components in the system (second law of thermodynamics).

HS-PS3–5: Develop and use a model of two objects interacting through electronic or magnetic fields to illustrate the forces between objects and the changes in energy of the objects due to interaction.

## Learning Progression: Science, High School, Energy

| Standard: Energy | Recall | Skills and Concepts | Strategic Thinking and Reasoning | Extended Thinking |
|---|---|---|---|---|
| HS-PS3–1 | | | CREATE a computational model to CALCULATE the change in energy of one component in a system when the change in energy of the other component(s) and energy flows in and out of the system are known. | |
| HS-PS3–2 | | DEVELOP and USE models to ILLUSTRATE that energy at the macroscopic scale can be accounted for as a combination of energy associated with the motions of particles (objects) and energy associated with the relative position of particles (objects). | | |
| HS-PS3–3 | | | DESIGN, BUILD, and REFINE a device that works within given constraints to convert one form of energy into another form of energy. | |
| HS-PS3–4 | | | PLAN and CONDUCT an investigation to PROVIDE evidence that the transfer of thermal energy when two components of different temperatures are combined within a closed system results in a more uniform energy distribution among the components in the system (second law of thermodynamics). | |
| HS-PS3–5 | | DEVELOP and USE a model of two objects interacting through electronic or magnetic fields to ILLUSTRATE the forces between objects and the changes in energy of the objects due to interaction. | | |

# APPENDIX G

## Second-Grade Math Learning Progression Example

|  | Webb's Depth of Knowledge (DOK) |
|---|---|
| Level 1 | Recall and Reproduction |
| Descriptor | Recall of a fact, information, or procedure |
| Level 2 | Skills and Concepts |
| Descriptor | Use of information, conceptual knowledge, procedures, two or more steps, etc. |
| Level 3 | Short-Term Strategic Thinking |
| Descriptor | Requires reasoning, developing a plan or sequence of steps; has some complexity; more than one possible answer |
| Level 4 | Extended Thinking |
| Descriptor | Requires an investigation; time to think and process multiple conditions of the problem or task |

# MATH SAMPLE

## Common Core State Standards for Math, Number and Operations in Base 10, Grade 2

2.NBT.1: Understand that the three digits of a three-digit number represent amounts of hundreds, tens, and ones.

2.NBT.1a: 100 can be thought of as a bundle of ten tens—called a "hundred."

2.NBT.1b: The numbers 100, 200, 300, 400, 500, 600, 700, 800, 900 refer to one, two, three, four, five, six, seven, eight, and nine hundreds (and 0 tens and 0 ones).

2.NBT.2: Count within 1,000: skip-count by 5s, 10s, and 100s.

2.NBT.3: Read and write numbers to 1,000 using base-ten numerals, number names, and expanded form.

2.NBT.4: Compare two three-digit numbers based on meanings of the hundreds, tens, and ones digits, using >, =, < symbols to record the results of comparisons.

2.NBT.5: Fluently add and subtract within 100 using strategies based on place value, properties of operations, and/or the relationship between addition and subtraction.

2.NBT.6: Add up to four two-digit numbers using strategies based on place value and properties.

2.NBT.7: Add and subtract within 1000, using concrete models or drawings and strategies based on place value, properties of operations, and/or the relationship between addition and subtraction. Relate the strategy to a written method. Understand that in adding or subtracting three-digit numbers, one adds or subtracts hundreds and hundreds, tens and tens, ones and ones; and sometimes it is necessary to compose or decompose tens and hundreds.

2.NBT.8: Mentally add 10 or 100 to a given number 100–900, and mentally subtract 10 or 100 from a given number 100–900.

2.NBT.9: Explain why addition and subtraction strategies work, using place value and the properties of operations.

## Learning Progression: Math, Number and Operations in Base 10, Grade 2

| Standard NBT | Recall | Skills and Concepts | Strategic Thinking and Reasoning | Extended Thinking |
|---|---|---|---|---|
| 2.NBT.1 | UNDERSTAND that the three digits of a three-digit number represent amounts of hundreds, tens, and ones. | | | |
| 2.NBT.1a | 100 can be thought of as a bundle of ten tens—called a "hundred." | | | |
| 2.NBT.1b | The numbers 100, 200, 300, 400, 500, 600, 700, 800, 900 refer to one, two, three, four, five, six, seven, eight, and nine hundreds (and 0 tens and 0 ones). | | | |

| Standard NBT | Recall | Skills and Concepts | Strategic Thinking and Reasoning | Extended Thinking |
|---|---|---|---|---|
| 2.NBT.2 | | COUNT within 1,000; skip-count by 5s, 10s, and 100s. | | |
| 2.NBT.3 | READ and WRITE numbers to 1,000 using base-ten numerals, number names, and expanded form. | | | |
| 2.NBT.4 | | | COMPARE two three digit-numbers based on meanings of the hundreds, tens, and ones digits, using >, =, < symbols to record the results of comparisons. | |
| 2.NBT.5 | FLUENTLY add and subtract within 100 using strategies based on place value, properties of operations, and/or the relationship between addition and subtraction. | | | |
| 2.NBT.6 | | ADD up to four two-digit numbers USING strategies based on place value and properties. | | |
| 2.NBT.7 | | ADD and SUBTRACT within 1,000, using concrete models or drawings and strategies based on place value, properties of operations, and/or the relationship between addition and subtraction; | | |

*(Continued)*

(Continued)

| Standard NBT | Recall | Skills and Concepts | Strategic Thinking and Reasoning | Extended Thinking |
|---|---|---|---|---|
| | | UNDERSTAND that in adding or subtracting three-digit numbers, one adds or subtracts hundreds and hundreds, tens and tens, ones and ones; and sometimes it is necessary to compose or decompose tens and hundreds. RELATE the strategy to a written method. | | |
| 2.NBT.8 | | MENTALLY ADD 10 or 100 to a given number 100–900, and mentally subtract 10 or 100 from a given number 100–900. | | |
| 2.NBT.9 | | | EXPLAIN why addition and subtraction strategies work, using place value and the properties of operations. | |

# APPENDIX H

## Fifth-Grade Personal Narrative Goal-Setting Sample

Date: _____

Topic: Personal Narrative
Standards: W.5.3, W.5.10
Tara Lindburg
Academy Charter School

| LEARNING GOAL |
| --- |
| Write a personal narrative that entertains the reader by sharing your thoughts and feelings about an important experience that has happened to you. W.5.3 |

| SUCCESS CRITERIA |
| --- |
| ❐ Orient your reader—introducing the story and characters W.5.3a |
| ❐ Organize (produce) a story with events that unfold naturally W.5.3b, W.5.4 |
| ❐ Use dialogue and description to develop strong characters W.5.b |
| ❐ Use a variety of transition words and phrases W.5.3c |
| ❐ Use words and phrases and sensory details to explain W.5.3d |
| ❐ Provide a conclusion that follows from the story W.5.3e |
| ❐ Develop and strengthen writing by planning, revising, editing, rewriting, or typing W.5.5 |
| ❐ Use technology to produce and publish writing W.5.6 |

| MIND FRAMES |
| --- |
| ❐ I won't quit. |
| ❐ I will make mistakes and learn from them. |
| ❐ I will expect much from myself. |
| ❐ I will listen to critique (opinions and ideas) for my writing. |

# Glossary

**Body of Evidence.** Multiple forms of evidence that prove student learning (i.e., pre- and post-assessment, performance assessments, homework, etc.).

**Class Credo.** A set of agreed-upon Learner Beliefs about learning that support collaboration, reflection, and risk-taking.

**Co-constructed Success Criteria.** The process of constructing the necessary criteria to successfully accomplish the Learning Intention with students.

**Delayed Feedback.** Feedback that is intended to deepen learning and is most effectively used after surface or foundational knowledge and understanding are in place.

**Depth of Knowledge (DOK).** A taxonomy of four levels developed by Norman L. Webb to analyze and align the cognitive demands of standards, grade-level expectations, and assessments.

**Feedback.** An exchange with the intent to nourish learning (**F**requent, **E**fficacious, **E**xchange-Oriented, **D**ifferentiated, **B**alanced, **A**ccurate, **C**riteria-Driven, **K**inesthetic).

**Fixed Mindset.** The belief that a person is born with a certain amount of intelligence or ability that defines or limits how much he or she is able to learn and achieve.

**Full Transfer.** The adoption of a strategy as a tool for learning from that of a teacher-owned instructional strategy to a student-owned Learner Strategy (i.e., note-taking, reading strategies, etc.).

**Growth Mindset.** The belief that intelligence and ability are malleable and can be developed as a result of effort and hard work.

**Handoff.** The moment in time when students are able to take ownership of their learning and become partners in learning with their teacher and peers.

**Immediate Feedback.** Feedback that is most effective when it takes place directly after a new idea or skill has been introduced and is intended to correct mistakes and misconceptions.

**Instructional Sequence.** A plan that describes how standards will be assessed and taught throughout the school year.

**Learner Beliefs.** The beliefs about oneself as a learner that underpin the actions of a learner.

**Learner Strategies.** Strategies that accelerate learning and can be applied to future learning experiences.

**Learner's True North.** Owning one's learning to achieve worthy goals.

**Learning Intention.** Represents what is intended for students to learn and is derived from the standards and the teacher's inference regarding what learning is needed at a particular moment in time.

**Learning Maps.** Visual representations of the Learning Intentions' most important concepts to be learned, and how they relate to one another.

**Learning Portfolio.** A body of student work that represents the journey toward meeting the Learning Intentions and the attainment of Learner Strategies.

**Learning Progressions.** A scaffold or progression of skills and concepts that exist within the standards and within any learning experience.

**Metacognition.** The practice of thinking about one's own thinking and learning.

**Mind Frames.** Beliefs or theories of practice about learning; beliefs that facilitate deep learning and align to research.

**Partial Transfer.** Occurs when students learn valuable skills from teacher-designed instructional strategies but do not fully adopt the strategy for future use (i.e., cooperative learning structures, etc.).

**Perceived Self-Efficacy.** One's belief in one's own abilities to achieve goals.

**Personalized Learning Goals.** Goals developed by students, based on the Learning Intentions paired with their results from the pre-assessment to establish goals that align to their needs and interests.

**Rapport + Responsiveness.** See *TRUST Model.*

**Rigor.** The level of complexity or cognitive demand of a standard or learning task.

**Self-Regulation.** The degree of influence over one's own motivation, thought processes, Learner Strategies, emotional states, and behavior.

**Structures.** See *TRUST Model.*

**Success Criteria.** Explicit criteria that define how to achieve the Learning Intentions.

**Talent.** See *TRUST Model.*

**Teacher's True North.** The skill and determination to empower all students with the wisdom and confidence to exceed expectations.

**Theories of Practice.** Words and actions that reveal deep-seated beliefs about teaching and learning.

**Time.** See *TRUST Model.*

**Transfer.** Adoption of strategies for learning from what is modeled in the classroom to one's own toolbox for learning.

**True North.** Internal compass that guides you successfully through life in order to reach worthy goals.

**TRUST Model (Talent, Rapport + Responsiveness, "Us" Factor, Structures, Time).** A framework of beliefs and actions that empowers teachers to partner with students to build ownership of learning.

> **Talent.** Deliberate actions to discover and develop the *talent for learning* in every learner.
>
> **Rapport + Responsiveness.** The ability to build relationships of trust and mutual respect and to respond or react appropriately to support learners.
>
> **"Us" Factor.** A shared belief that everyone can learn and everyone is a vital contributor to the learning process.
>
> **Structures.** The methods, procedures, and practices that enable students to be partners in the learning process and to own their learning.
>
> **Time.** The requirement of purposeful and intentional time dedicated to building collaborative relationships and developing Learner Beliefs and actions.

**"Us" Factor.** See *TRUST Model.*

# List of Figures

## CHAPTER 5. LEARNING THROUGH EFFECTIVE FEEDBACK

## CHAPTER 6. RETRACING EVIDENCE TO PROVE AND EXTEND LEARNING

# CHAPTER 7. RETRACING AND EXTENDING THE PROCESS: A SUMMARY TO GUIDE TEACHERS AND LEADERS

7.1a Defining the Journey Template*

7.1b Learning on the Journey Template*

7.1c Retracing and Extending the Journey Template*

7.2 Teacher's Internal Compass Personalized

7.3 Learners' Internal Compass Personalized

7.4 Teacher's and Learner's Internal Compasses Aligned

7.5 The Teacher's Internal Compass: Getting Ready to Take Action*

7.6 Leader's Internal Compass: True North

7.7 Leader's TRUST Model for Planning: Building Collaborative Relationships*

7.8 Partnering With Students to Build Ownership of Learning: Planning Template*

7.9 Effective Feedback for Adult Learners*

*Items marked by an asterisk (\*) are available electronically, as blank templates.*

Visit the companion website at
**www.corwin.com/partneringwithstudents**
for additional resources.

# References

Absolum, M. (2006). *Clarity in the classroom.* Auckland, New Zealand: Hodder Education.

Absolum, M. (2010). *Clarity in the classroom: Using formative assessment for building learner-focused relationships.* Winnipeg, MB, Canada: Portage & Main Press.

Ainsworth, L. (2010). *Rigorous curriculum design: How to create curriculum units of study that align standards, instruction, and assessment.* Englewood, CO: Lead + Learn Press.

Ainsworth, L., & Viegut, D. (2015). *Common formative assessment 2.0: How teacher teams intentionally align standards, instruction, and assessment.* Thousand Oaks, CA: Corwin.

Bandura, A. (1977). Self-efficacy: Toward a unifying theory of behavioral change. *Psychological Review, 84*(2), 191–215.

Bandura, A. (1994). *Self-efficacy.* In V. S. Ramachaudran (Ed.), *Encyclopedia of human behavior* (Vol. 4, pp. 71–81). New York: Academic Press.

Bandura, A. (1997). *Self-efficacy: The exercise of control.* Freeman, NY: Worth Publishers. Macmillan Education.

Black, P., & Wiliam, D. (1998). Inside the black box: Raising standards through classroom assessment. *Phi Delta Kappan, 80*(2), 139–144, 146–148.

Boch, F., & Piolat, A. (2005). Note taking and learning: A summary of research. *The WAC Journal 16.*

Bridgeland, J. M., Dilulio, J. J., & Morison, K. B. (2006). The silent epidemic: Perspectives from high school dropouts. Civic Enterprises. Retrieved from https://docs.gatesfoundation.org/Documents/thesilentepidemic3-06FINAL.pdf

Clarke, S. (2001). *Unlocking formative assessment: Practical strategies for enhancing pupils' learning in the primary classroom.* London, England: Hodder Education.

Clarke, S. (2005). *Formative assessment in the secondary classroom.* London, England: Hodder Education.

Clarke, S. (2008). *Active learning through formative assessment.* London, England: Hodder Education.

Cognition Education. (2013). *Visible learning plus: Foundation workbook.* Thousand Oaks, CA: Corwin.

Cornelius-White, J. (2007). Learner-centered teacher–student relationships are effective: A meta-analysis. *Review of Educational Research, 77*(1), 113–143.

Cornelius-White, J., & Harbaugh, A. P. (2010). *Learner-centered instruction: Building relationships for student success.* Thousand Oaks, CA: Sage.

Csikszentmihalyi, M. (1990). *Flow: The psychology of optimal experience.* New York: HarperCollins Publishers.

Cushman, K. (2005). *Sent to the principal: Students talk about making high schools better.* Providence, RI: New Generation Press.

Dean, C., Hubbell, E., Pitler, H., & Stone, B. (2012). *Classroom instruction that works: Research-based strategies for increasing student achievement* (2nd ed.). Alexandria, VA: ASCD.

Dweck, C. (2006). *Mindset: The new psychology of success.* New York: Ballantine Press.

Dweck, C. (2007). The perils and promises of praise. *Educational Leadership, 65*(2), 34–39.

Dweck, C. (2010). Mind-sets and equitable education. *Principal Leadership, 20,* 26–29.

Faber, A., & Mazlish, E. (1995). *How to talk so kids can learn: At home and in school.* New York: Scribner.

Fendick, F. (1990). The correlation between teacher clarity of communication and student achievement gain: A meta-analysis. University of Florida. Retrieved from http://books.google.com/books?id=kT-8tgAACAAJ

Fisher, D., & Frey, N. (2011). *The formative assessment action plan: Practical steps to more successful teaching and learning.* Alexandria, VA: ASCD.

Freiberg, J. H., & Lamb, S. M. (2009). Dimensions of person-centered classroom management. *Theory Into Practice, 48*(2), 99–105. Copyright © The College of Education and Human Ecology, The Ohio State University. doi:10.1080/00405840902776228

Gallimore, R., & Tharp, R. (2004). What a coach can teach a teacher, 1975–2004: Reflections and reanalysis of John Wooden's teaching practices. *The Sports Psychologist, 18,* 119–137. Retrieved from http://bit.ly/1zkKD74

Gallup Student Poll. (2013). Gallup, Inc. Retrieved from http://www.gallupstudentpoll.com/174020/2013-gallup-student-poll-overall-report.aspx

George, B., & Sims, P. (2007). *True north: Discover your authentic leadership.* San Francisco, CA: Jossey-Bass.

Hattie, J. A. (2003). Who says formative assessment matters? Formative and summative interpretations of assessment information. University of Auckland, School of Education. Retrieved from https://cdn.auckland.ac.nz/assets/education/hattie/docs/formative-and-summative-assessment-(2003).pdf

Hattie, J. A. (2009). *Visible learning: A synthesis of over 800 meta-analyses relating to achievement.* New York: Routledge.

Hattie, J. A. (2011). Keynote address. 90/90/90 Schools Summit. Leadership and Learning Center, Charlotte, NC.

Hattie, J. A. (2012). *Visible learning for teachers: Maximizing impact on teachers.* New York: Routledge.

Hattie, J. A. (2013). Understanding learning: Lessons for learning, teaching, and research. Research conference 2013. Retrieved from http://research.acer.edu.au/cgi/viewcontent.cgi?article=1207&context=research_conference

Hattie, J. A., & Timperley, H. (2007). The power of feedback. *American Educational Research Association.* Thousand Oaks, CA: Sage. Retrieved from http://rer.sagepub.com/cgi/content/abstract/77/1/81

Heritage, M. (2010). *Formative assessment: Making it happen in the classroom.* Thousand Oaks, CA: Corwin.

Hill, J. D., & Flynn, K. M. (2006). *Classroom instruction that works with English language learners.* Alexandria, VA: ASCD.

Jones, B. R. (2014). *Imperative leadership: What must be done for students to succeed.* Englewood, CO: Lead + Learn Press.

Kagan, S. (1994). *Cooperative learning.* San Clemente, CA: Resources for Teachers, Inc.

King, S. (2002). *On writing: A memoir of the craft.* New York: Pocket Books.

Knight, J. (2013). *High-impact instruction: A framework for great teaching.* Thousand Oaks, CA: Corwin.

Kouzes, J. M., & Posner, B. Z. (2014). *Turning adversity into opportunity.* San Francisco, CA: Jossey-Bass.

Marzano, R. J. (2003). *What works in schools: Translating research into action.* Alexandria, VA: ASCD.

McCombs, B. L., & Miller, L. (2007). *Learner-centered classroom practices and assessments: Maximizing student motivation, learning, and achievement.* Thousand Oaks, CA: Corwin.

Measures of Effective Teaching (MET) Project: Policy and Practice Brief. (2012). Asking students about teaching: Student perception surveys and their implementation. Retrieved from http://www.metproject.org/reports.php

My Voice National Student Report. (2013). Portland, ME: Quaglia Institute for Student Aspirations. Retrieved from www.qisa.org

National Governors Association Center for Best Practices, and Council of Chief State School Officers. (2010a). *Common Core state standards for English language arts and literacy in history/social studies, science, and technical subjects.* Washington, DC. Retrieved from http://www.corestandards.org/ELA-Literacy/

National Governors Association Center for Best Practices, and Council of Chief State School Officers. (2010b). *Common Core state standards for mathematics.* Washington, DC. Retrieved from http://www.corestandards.org/Math/

New Generation Science Standards. (2013). Achieve, Inc. Retrieved from http://www.nextgenscience.org/next-generation-science-standards

Nilson, L. B. (2013). *Creating self-regulated learners: Strategies to strengthen students' self-awareness and learning skills.* Sterling, VA: Stylus Publishing, LLC.

Nuthall, G. (2007). *The hidden lives of learners.* Wellington, New Zealand: NZCER Press.

Oxford Dictionaries. (2014). Retrieved from http://www.oxforddictionaries.com/us

Pollock, J. E. (2012). *Feedback: The hinge that joins teaching and learning.* Thousand Oaks, CA: Corwin.

Popham, W. J. (2008). *Transformative assessment.* Alexandria, VA: ASCD.

Quaglia, R. J. (2014). Keynote address. Corwin author consultant retreat. Rancho Palos Verdes, CA.

Quaglia, R. J., & Corso, M. J. (2014). *Student voice: The instrument of change.* Thousand Oaks, CA: Corwin.

Quaglia Institute for Students Aspirations. (2013). *My Voice National Student Report, Grades 6–12.* Retrieved from http://www.qisa.org/

Reeves, D. B. (2006). *The learning leader: How to focus school improvement for better results.* Alexandria, VA: ASCD.

Refocus: Looking at assessment for learning. (2005). Edmonton, Canada: Alberta Assessment Consortium. Retrieved from www.acc.ab.ca

Ritchhart, R., Church, M., & Morrison, K. (2011). *Making thinking visible: How to promote engagement, understanding, and independence for all learners.* San Francisco, CA: Jossey-Bass.

Robinson, V. (2011). *Student-centered leadership*. San Francisco, CA: Jossey-Bass.

Robinson, V., Hohepa, M., & Lloyd, C. (2009). *School leadership and student outcomes: Identifying what works and why*. Wellington: New Zealand Ministry of Education. Retrieved from www.educationcounts.govt.nz/publications/series/2515/60169/60170

Stiggins, R. J., Arter, J. A., Chappuis, J., & Chappuis, S. (2006). *Classroom assessment for student learning: Using it right, doing it well*. Upper Saddle River, NJ: Pearson.

Stone, D., & Heen, S. (2014). *Thanks for the feedback: The science and art of receiving feedback well*. New York: The Penguin Group LLC.

Webb, N. L. (2005). Alignment, depth of knowledge, and change. Wisconsin Center for Education Research. Florida Educational Research Association fiftieth annual meeting, November 17, 2005. Retrieved from http://facstaff.wcer.wisc.edu/normw/

Wiggins, G., & McTighe, J. (2005). *Understanding by design* (expanded 2nd ed.). Alexandria, VA: ASCD.

Wiliam, D. (2011). *Embedded formative assessment*. Bloomington, IN: Solution Tree Press.

Zegarac, G. (2013). Know thy impact: Teaching, learning, and leading: A conversation with John Hattie. *Conversation, 4*(2).

Zubizarreta, J. (2008). The learning portfolio: A powerful idea for significant learning. Manhattan, KS: The Idea Factory. Idea paper no. 44.

# Index